D0773011

# MUSICAL CHAIRS

## A 76-Year-Old's Quest to Learn
## Every Instrument in the Orchestra

# MUSICAL CHAIRS

## A 76-Year-Old's Quest to Learn
## Every Instrument in the Orchestra

## James Mitchell

www.BookpressPublishing.com

Any requests or questions for the author should be submitted to him directly at musicalchairsbook@gmail.com or visit his website at jamesmitchellbooks.com.

Readers should be aware that Internet sites offered as citations and/or sources for further information may have changed or disappeared between the time this was written and when it is read.

Published in Des Moines, Iowa, by:
Bookpress Publishing
P.O. Box 71532, Des Moines, IA 50325
www.BookpressPublishing.com

**Publisher's Cataloging-in-Publication Data**

Names: Mitchell, James, 1943-, author.
Title: Musical Chairs : A 76-year-old's quest to learn every instrument in the orchestra / James Mitchell.
Description: Des Moines, IA: Bookpress Publishing, 2023.
Identifiers: LCCN: 2023900450 | ISBN: 978-1-947305-65-6
Subjects: LCSH Mitchell, James, 1943- . | Musical instruments--Instruction and study. | Practicing (Music) | Music--Instruction and study--Psychological aspects. | Humor. | Self-actualization (Psychology). | BISAC BIOGRAPHY & AUTOBIORAPHY / Personal Memoirs | MUSIC / Musical Instruments / General | HUMOR / General | SELF-HELP / Personal Growth / General
Classification: LCC MT1 .M58 2023 | DDC 784.193/092--dc23

First Edition
*Printed in the United States of America*
10 9 8 7 6 5 4 3 2 1

*To my wife, Doyen, whose patience rivals that of the saints, and whose encouragement kept me going through untold screeches and squawks.*

# CONTENTS

# Warm-Up

My wife, Doyen, and I were on our way back from a road trip to Tucson, in about hour ten of a fifteen-hour drive home to Colorado. We had been quiet for a while, enjoying the piñon country of northern New Mexico, when I blurted out, "Here's an idea...."

That is always a sure sign for my wife to tighten her seatbelt since, in the past, it has led to things such as building a covered wagon to take family trips on the Oregon Trail and spending Christmas in a log cabin at forty below zero.

But this was different. I had been antsy for some time, looking for a project to dig into and not coming up with anything worthwhile. Suddenly, without warning, it came to me in a rush, completely formed, amidst that desolate New Mexico landscape: I would play all the instruments in the orchestra.

I am not a musician, but I have a lifelong love of classical music and am always in awe listening to those who make the music I love.

How many of us, I thought, would want the experience of feeling a bow in our hand, or keys or valves under our fingers, and the glorious sensation of making music?

*"You know I love classical music, right?" I ask Doyen.*

*"Yes," Doyen says, her voice rising to a lingering question.*

*"I think I'd like to play all the instruments in the orchestra."*

*"All of them," she states flatly, the words catching in her throat.*

*"Well, almost all of them," I reply.*

*Humoring me, she says, "And how are you going to do that?"*

*"It's simple. I'll just take lessons."*

*"That's simple?"*

*"Yes, why not?"*

*"Jim," Doyen says in a soothing and placating voice, "you're seventy-six."*

For me, it is always good to have a goal. It gives life direction and leads to self-improvement, knowledge, motivation, achievement, and, most of all, a sense of fulfillment. But you can't just start off in some random direction and hope that somehow, with a bit of luck or serendipity, you will reach your goal. You need a plan. It is like taking a road trip. If you don't have a destination in mind and a road map, how will you know when you get there?

With that statement, I have clearly staked out a battleground between *process* people and *results* people.

To a process purist, life is about the journey, not the end result. The result folks focus hard on what they have when they are done. Yet neither approach needs to be taken in absolute terms, one to the mutual exclusion of the other. Certainly, you can enjoy the trip along the way to your destination, even revel in it, take detours, explore different routes, and take as much time as your life will allow. That is process. You still have a goal and a plan of how to get there. It gives you a sense of purpose. That is results.

My goal is to play (almost) every instrument in the symphony orchestra. Not to mastery—that would be unrealistic, and at least for me, patently unachievable. Not to mastery, but to competency.

True, one man's competency is another man's abject failure or stunning success. It is rather subjective. But this is not a test. This is a journey (n.b.: process people) and, at least at the outset, an achievable goal (a nod to results people). For me, the idea will be to play excerpts from the classical music repertory with a high degree of fluency, tone, and interpretation, in a reasonably listenable fashion, on eleven of the orchestra's most iconic instruments.

To wit:

*Violin*

*Viola*

*Cello*

*Bass*

*Clarinet*

*Flute*

*Oboe*

*Bassoon*

*Trumpet*

*Trombone*

*French horn*

If life were an endless continuum without the measurement of time, I could dedicate myself to this project and move from one instrument to another only when I had achieved the goal—no risk of failure there. But time is measured, and it is not unlimited. Enter another challenge to make this enterprise more interesting and unpredictable, yet doable. I will limit myself to just twelve lessons on each instrument, about three months. Will that be enough time and lessons to reach the goal of a high degree of competency, tone, and interpretation? What if I do not reach the goal? What if I simply cannot play a double reed instrument or the devilishly difficult French horn?

What if I can't find someone to take me on as a student when they know they will only have me for twelve lessons? What if the sky falls?

Eschewing the Chicken Little metaphor, I realize that

right now, there is no answer to those questions. Only time will tell.

My musical education started with the piano when I was ten, living with my brother and parents in New York City. I was not very good at the piano, but it gave me a grounding in reading music, rhythm, harmony, and a hint of what dedication it would take to really become a musician. I liked the lessons, and was fascinated by my old-world Viennese teacher whose West Side apartment was less of a music studio and more of what you would expect Sigmund Freud's consultation room to be like: dimly lit, with dark, heavy drapes, Turkish carpets, table lamps with teardrop crystals dangling from their dusty fabric shades, and an overstuffed settee with a festoon of brass upholstery tacks curling like a necklace up an arm, across the back and down all around the curved edges of the seat.

Sitting next to me on the piano bench, Mrs. Froenlich was always gentle and understanding, but her patience was belied by the increasingly frequent brushing back of wisps of her white-streaked auburn hair. Her coif was piled high and twisted by who knows what feats of prestidigitation into a spiraling mound perched on top of her head. It looked to my ten-year-old eyes much like a giant sticky bun. By the end of a particularly exasperating lesson, at least for her, she would be batting away the wisps of hair like so many flies at a summer picnic.

More musically influential than Mrs. Froenlich though, was my mother, who played the piano throughout my childhood years. She had an old upright and later, a spinet, although she deserved something better. She was good. Not "concert grand" good, but good enough to have had a better instrument. Maybe a baby grand. She was partial to Chopin and played his waltzes and preludes well enough to leave an indelible auditory memory. I can still hear the old upright, with not the crispest of action and a piece of ivory missing from the middle D key, bending to the will of Mom as she nevertheless coaxed lovely music out of it. She was diminutive, maybe 5' and maybe 100 lbs., but she made Chopin ring out in our apartment.

I appreciate it more now than I did when I was a boy, when I was much more interested in baseball than just about anything else. After all, she was, to me, above all else, my mom. As long as she fulfilled that role, whatever else she did, no matter how accomplished she may have been at it, was secondary.

The piano wasn't the only instrument I played as a youth. I also took up the clarinet in junior high school but did not play it very well either, or at least not as well as I thought I should have.

This is indicative of a lifelong trait of mine. I often think I *should* be able to do something better than I *can*, which makes me alternate between frustration and disappointment on the one hand, and determination and a commitment to improve on the other. It is what psychologist Karen Horney calls "The Tyranny of the Shoulds." I should be able to do such and such. It can beat you up pretty badly if you let it, but the shoulds can also be a powerful motivator, keeping you on the road to improvement, as long as it stays on the safe side of tyranny.

The first decision I have to make on this project is where to start. Strings, woodwinds, or brass. Eleven instruments in all, each one with its own seductive power. Like the Sirens singing to Odysseus from their rocky island lair, the eleven instruments beckon to me to let them be the first. To which will I give my orchestral virginity?

The woodwinds all have solo voices that often get the most beautiful passages in a composition.

The brass are, at times, so stunningly bold that they will not be denied.

And the strings can blend or stand out, lead or follow.

Because I want to tackle the hardest when I am at my freshest and most enthusiastic, I decide to go with what I know the least about: The strings.

I seek counsel from musician friends as to which one might be the best for an absolute novice, beginner, and know-nothing wannabe. Of course, as you might expect, each one has a different opinion, and sometimes two or three:

1. The violin, because the notes are really close together, you can cover four notes on the finger board without changing the position of your left hand.

*Not the violin, for the same reason; the notes are so close together that it makes it harder to play the ones you want to play.*

2. The double bass because it's big and easier to find the notes because you can see where to place your fingers.

*Not the double bass because the left hand has to stretch so far searching for the notes, it is like watching a crab scurrying up and down the fingerboard looking for a meal. And it is too big. It is the Sumo wrestler of the orchestra and too much to handle for a beginner.*

3. The cello should be first because, as one friend puts it, "It's the Goldilocks of the strings. Just the right size."

*No, not the cello. It can cause tennis elbow and is a killer on your back.*

4. Nobody suggests the viola, and I just let it ride.

I think about it and try to picture myself with each of the strings. It comes down to whether I want to be conspicuous, lugging around a sizeable cello case or an even bigger bass, or inconspicuous, hugging a much smaller violin or viola protectively to my chest as I go places. Wavering back and forth, I narrow it down incongruously to the violin or the double bass.

For some, the violin might be the better choice, but after some reflection, probably not for me. For me, it is like carpentry. If you are building a barn with rough wood, where cracks between the boards are OK, and there is lots of room for error, bang in the nails and call it a day, that is for me.

If, on the other hand, you want to make a fine piece of furniture, matching the grain and leaving no evidence of joinery, better leave me at home. So, the double bass is my barn. That's where I will start.

Hopefully, over time, I will also be able to build fine

furniture, as long as you don't look too closely.

Having decided on the double bass first, it is natural that I will then move up the ladder to the mid-range of the cello and viola, and then finish the strings with the high-pitched violin. That sequence seems to make sense, and I could use it as a template for the woodwinds and brass as well, start low and finish high. I have now picked a destination and have a map of how to get there. All I need now is the will, determination, and enough talent to enjoy my game of musical chairs through the orchestra.

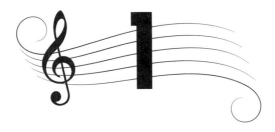

# The Double Bass

I have never in my life held a fretless stringed instrument in my hand, with one exception, which is part of the reason I am starting with the double bass.

In high school, the orchestra was not the most popular elective, but some of my friends were in it, and they needed to have one double bass player to fill out the orchestra. *Heck, thought I, it only has four strings, and it is at the very back of the orchestra; why not?* So I said yes and signed on.

The first day of rehearsal, everyone showed up in the music room with their instruments. I lugged in the double bass from a musty school closet, which it shared with faculty coats, unmatched folding chairs, old file boxes with faded, curling labels, and probably a few scurrying furry things.

Making sure that I was as far away from the conductor as possible, I settled onto a tall stool and leaned the bass against my knee. I looked the part but did not have the slightest idea how to tune the bass, much less find any notes with my left hand or bow it properly with my right. But I was a pretty good mimic and went through the motions of the bass players I had seen at Carnegie Hall and the Metropolitan Opera. I looked seriously at the score in front of me, counted the measures to know when the bass was supposed to come in and cut off, and fiddled with the bow well enough to almost touch the strings yet not actually make any sound whatsoever. Nobody ever caught on, and I enjoyed the only time I was ever in an orchestra. I think the conductor must have been mostly deaf.

Given a second chance these many years later to actually learn the bass, I set out on my maiden voyage.

Finding a music store to rent a double bass is easy. Explaining why I want to rent one for just three months, then go on to another instrument, and then another, each for three months at a time is not so easy.

The owner of the music store, a cross between Harpo Marx and Woody Allen, used all the quizzical expressions you might imagine those other two using as he cocked his head this way and that, raised his eyebrows, wrinkled his nose, looked to the heavens, and finally threw up his hands and told his sales clerk, "This guy's nuts, but give him what he wants," then sotto voce, "Cash only, no credit."

So, with that questionable background and introduction,

I nevertheless embrace the double bass. But it is not easy to embrace a double bass. When you first meet the bass up close, it is a monster. It is a bit intimidating, and more or less like unexpectedly running into a Green Bay Packers linebacker. Unless you are said linebacker, the bass is taller than you are, wider than you are, weighs more than that overstuffed suitcase you took with you on a month-long trip to Europe, and is about as easy to handle as a folding beach chair.

Nevertheless, I have the instrument. Now I need lessons. I get the name and number of a bass teacher from a local music school. Not a lot of serious research or vetting goes into it, but who am I to be picky? My thinking is that it may be difficult to find anyone at all who is willing to take on an older adult student for just twelve lessons. Yet, I want to have a good teacher.

I have taught a little bit as an adjunct professor and have been taught a lot. My wife is a fabulous teacher. In fact, the way she explains ordinary things to me is filled with background detail and step-by-step sequences that lead to unambiguous understanding. It is very thorough but sometimes can also be a little exasperating, as in when all I want to know is if the mail has come in yet, and learn that the *Post-Office-changed-its-schedule-and-that-our-mail-carrier-now-has-us-last-on-his-route-rather-than-first-the-way-it-used-to-be-but-it-might-change-again-when-the-regular-driver-comes-back-or-if-the-sub-gets-used-to-the-route-and-does-it-faster.*

Yes, but did the mail come in yet?

My wife hastens to say that that is not the way she

explains things to her normal students, only the "special" ones.

Not wanting to waste time, I called the bass teacher recommended by the music school the next day. With some trepidation, I explain the project to the man on the other end of the phone, and he says, "Never done anything like that before, but it's an interesting experiment. Why not?" I am relieved at not being summarily dismissed, but I am still apprehensive about what will happen.

The night before my first bass lesson, I dream I am playing the bass in a dark room and getting it to make that rich rumbling sound that vibrates into your chest. There is nobody around, but two tickets are lying on a stool in a bright spotlight, and they are like World Series or NBA playoff tickets. They are very colorful, but instead of a picture of Clayton Kershaw or LeBron James, there is James Saxon, the diminutive, bald, former principal bass player of the Denver Symphony Orchestra. A minor star in his own right, he probably never dreamed he would make it to the Big Show. Not even in a dream. There is conflict in the dream, mirroring mine about what will happen when I actually start playing an instrument.

Hoping that the "experiment," as my teacher called it, turns out better than Dr. Frankenstein's, I open the door two days later with bow in hand and welcome my first teacher, Byron Dudrey, for my inaugural bass lesson.

Byron is well-prepared, and we launch into the basics of playing the bass right away. He is calm and understanding, using gentle suggestions and patient encouragement to egg me on.

Byron and I talk about what melody I want to play as a goal to strive for. At one point, I thought it would be interesting to learn the same excerpt from the same piece on each instrument and see how different, easier, or more difficult the piece would be as I worked my way around the orchestra. Then we hit on the idea of choosing a different, iconic, or at least typical excerpt from the symphonic repertoire for each instrument.

Maybe the *Meditation* from Massenet's *Thaïs* for the violin, *Peter and the Wolf* for the bassoon, the Mozart *Concerto in C Major* for the oboe, Bruch's *Kol Nidre* for the cello, and the haunting melody from the third movement of Brahm's *Symphony No. 1* for the French horn. The ideas keep flowing, and the conversation is stimulating. OK, they are all good ideas, but I have a double bass in front of me. What about the double bass? Byron's eyes widen as if to say, "You don't know?" I widen my eyes right back at him expectantly as if to say, "Go on, go on."

"Why, it's Beethoven's *Ninth*," he says. "The *Ode to Joy*. That theme is introduced by the double basses. You have to change positions to do it the way Beethoven wrote it, but that's the one."

So, we have our goal, and the lessons continue.

I decide to use the German bow technique rather than the French because it is a lot different from the bow hold of the other strings I will encounter and will make the experience more unique. With the German bow, you hold it somewhat like a saw, and if, in my mind's eye, I picture a beefy German butcher working away on a pork chop, I hope I may be forgiven.

To spare Doyen the auditory damage that might come from listening to me play, I move the bass into my home office, but the light there is not ideal for practicing. There is too much furniture and stuff, things collected from travels, and a small forest of plants in the corner over which hangs a flight cage for finches. Or finch, as it is now housing only one zebra finch, a male, who, while I was away on a trip, managed, in dramatic Greek tragedy fashion, to kill his wife and daughter. I am planning to offer him for free on Craigslist.

There is also a desk for computer work and writing and an almost too comfortable chair and footstool for reading. Bookshelves, an exercise bike, a printer, and a credenza round out the mélange of furniture, leaving little space for a 6'2" upright bass to lie down. And lie down it must so that it doesn't fall down. It lies there somewhat like a voluptuous odalisque awaiting the call of a muse.

The lighting is great for reading in the chair or for computer work at the desk, but not good at all for reading music while sitting on a stool in front of the birdcage. What to do? My old, spindly, three-legged music stand is too wobbly for me to attach a light. More than once, I have sent music, notes, resin, pencil, and bow flying at the mere touch of a sleeve or shoulder. Camping headlamp to the rescue. It is perfect. Adjustable angle, brilliantly bright, and with a comfortable elastic headband to keep it focused on the music. I may look more like a coal miner than a musician, but it works.

I practice regularly, but because my lessons are a week

apart, I too often find myself practicing wrong, getting stymied, and finding the solution to the problem only when Byron shows up the next week and sets me straight. He is a fine teacher. He observes and offers specific solutions to the problems I am having. Not cookie-cutter, one-size-fits-all solutions, but what I at this moment in time, at this point of development, need corrected in order to move on.

Then one day, he shakes his head and says, "Something's just not right; something is wrong." That's strong language from Byron. I know I am not sounding great, but is it so bad that it is just plain wrong? But he is not looking at me. He is looking at the bass. He takes it from me and says, "It's the instrument. It's not set up right."

We lay the bass down on its back as if it were at an accident scene and in critical condition. We, two EMTs, are doing our best to save it. Cautioning me never to lay a double bass on its back unless it is an emergency, which this must be, we loosen the tuning pegs so we can realign the bridge with the fingerboard. "Can't loosen the strings too much," says Byron, "or without enough tension from front to back, the sound post inside the bass may dislodge, and then we'll be in real trouble. You need a special tool to reach in and prop it back up, and you have to have that peg. It is what carries the vibrations from the front to the back."

It is like resetting a bone, measuring the distance from the f-holes to the bottom of the bridge legs, and aligning the bridge so it is level with the cross mark on the f-holes. The operation is a success, and the tone, especially on what was a raspy and buzzing G string, is now mellow and easier to bow.

So it wasn't only my playing.

This close encounter makes me wonder how this large vibration box came about in the first place. Early examples showed up in the 1500s with almost as many different sizes as there were tunings, which some scholars say numbered around fifty. The four-string E-A-D-G tuning of today wasn't standardized until the early 20th century.

There were some odd variants, including six-string double basses and three-string double basses, fretted double basses that used gut for the frets, and a 17th-century model that was eight feet tall, the height of a standard ceiling today. Later, in 1849, Jean-Baptiste Vuillaume built a thirteen-foot-tall bass that required two people to play. It seems to me that one belonged in the circus.

The instrument might have disappeared altogether if not for the invention of wound strings. The early gut strings were so thick that they made it very hard to play and keep in tune. The basses of the day also did not project well. Winding copper wire around the gut allowed the strings to be smaller and hold their tuning better. These were later replaced in the 20th century by all steel strings, which give the instrument the resonance we hear now in the concert hall. Yet even today, there is a difference between the standard, or orchestral tuning, and the tuning that a soloist uses. For concertos and chamber works, soloists tune a full step higher and use different strings to give the instrument a more upfront, clear, and bright tone.

Until Domenico Dragonetti (1763-1846) came on the scene, the basses played, or doubled, the cello part but an octave lower. Dragonetti was a virtuoso, so extraordinary that it is said he could play violin parts on the bass. He was also a friend of Beethoven, and it was Dragonetti's influence that began to emancipate the double bass from its role of merely doubling the cello part to having its own harmonic line.

My lessons continue, and we are solely focused on the *Ode to Joy*. It feels stale from time to time because I am not working on anything else, but it's still hard to get it right. Most projects have a distinctly defined beginning, middle, and end, which mark the progress toward completion and, ultimately, accomplishment. The bass lessons, however, seem more like a continuum without definition.

Because of this sensation, I don't know if I am really learning how to play the bass. My goal is to play *Ode to Joy*, that simple yet impelling theme in the final movement of Beethoven's *Ninth*. But I do not play it the way Beethoven wrote it. He wrote it with three different hand position shifts, and I play it with only two, and it's taken me almost three months to get even that far. *Is not playing it according to the original score cheating?* I can't completely convince myself one way or the other. What I do know is that with non-music commitments breaking up the continuity of learning something new, it has taken a lot longer than I expected.

As we are near the twelfth lesson, it doesn't sound bad. I can even get the bass to ring out and resonate, but something inside me is missing. I don't feel the flush of success I had anticipated—no exultation at completing my first foray into the depths of the orchestra. My imagination doesn't take me into sitting on my stool in the bass section in a concert hall alongside other tuxedoed musicians as the hushed audience listens to us rumble out the *Ode to Joy*.

I have to admit to feeling a vague sense of disappointment. *Is this all there is after twelve weeks of lessons? Will all the others end the same way?* I remember thinking to myself at the end of a symphony concert how the musicians seemed to be in a hurry to pack up and leave, maybe to beat the traffic home. It perplexed me that they did not feel the same emotions that the audience felt listening to them.

Granted, I have learned a lot and enjoyed the *process*, so there is value in that. Yet, I am at least equal parts a *results* person, meaning that I see the double bass "glass" as being half full and half empty at the same time. It is a bit confusing. I am certain there is more emotion to be felt and more satisfaction to be had in going from zero ability to reasonably listenable. And I have felt that emotion and satisfaction singing folk songs and Christmas carols with friends.

So, it is with an inconclusive scratch of my head that I say goodbye to good-natured Byron and prepare to return the rented double bass to the music store, anticipating with a smile what reaction I might get when I tell the Harpo/Woody owner that we had to perform surgery on his instrument.

# The Cello

One summer many years ago, I was sitting in the front row under a tent at the Aspen Music Festival, back in the days when it was still a pretty casual affair. With a day pass, you could wander into one of the music tents, find an empty folding chair, sit down, and hear some fine classical music.

I did not know what was on the schedule that day and got there early with a book I was reading. I settled in and was engrossed in the book as the musicians came in and fiddled with their instruments and arranged their music stands. I was still reading when the concertmaster stood, the oboe sounded its A, and the orchestra tuned up. There was a smattering of polite applause as the cello soloist walked onto the stage and sat down. It was not until he bowed the opening phrases of Saint-Saëns's *Concerto No. 1 in D Major* that my head snapped up, the book fell between my knees, and I became immediately transfixed by the emotion and passion of the youthful cellist. Of course, you can guess the rest of the story. It was a very young Yo-Yo Ma, and there was no doubt even then that I was hearing someone extraordinary.

The cello has a soulful sound, and its timbre is considered to be more like the human voice than any other instrument. If you sit near a cello at a chamber music concert or are actually playing one, you can feel the vibrations in your bones. This human quality of the cello has always appealed to me, and I am looking forward to trying to have some good conversations with it.

After the oversized proportions of the bass, I am also looking forward to something more to scale with my proportions.

I am not disappointed, and I almost cannot believe how much easier it is to make progress compared to the double bass. It is probably because I cut my teeth on the double bass and can now chew more comfortably on the cello.

It may be like plowing an untilled field. It is a real struggle to break new ground. The earth seems to resist your effort, but each pass you make gets a little bit easier, more fluid, it takes less muscle, and you start working with the soil and not against it.

My teacher is different, too. Right from the start, Chris Abbot pushes me, frequently reminding me that in order to achieve my goal in just twelve lessons, we cannot do it the usual way. My bass teacher was kind, understanding, and gentle with me, as if he were handling a somewhat fragile vase. Chris, on the other hand, is stern and direct. She pounds me like a circus roustabout driving in a tent peg for The Big Top. She is not exactly dictatorial but brooks little disagreement and seems more like a 19th-century, ruler-wielding school-marm than a music teacher hailing from Milwaukee, which she is.

Chris is perceptive and burrows in on what I have to do to keep moving forward. She tells me that we are doing things she wouldn't normally do with a new student for six months to a year. I don't know what we are leaving out, and since I don't know what I don't know, I naively take it as a sort of compliment and just try to follow her lead.

To get the rich baritone sonority from the cello, you have to master the essentials of pitch and tone. The left hand works the strings and determines the pitch of the notes, and the right hand, with just the right amount of weight, speed, and direction on the bow, is responsible for the tone.

What makes the strings so challenging is that they demand two very different skill sets from the player. The left hand requires dexterity and highly developed fine motor skills, with fingers moving independently, and on the cello, vertically up and down the fingerboard all the time. While the left is doing its thing, the right hand is, to put it roughly, sawing back and forth horizontally on a completely different plane. It is the ultimate pat-your-head-and-rub-your-belly routine. Yet as different as these two maneuvers are, they have to be precisely coordinated all the time.

It is very different from the woodwinds and even the piano.

On those instruments, all the fingers on both hands are more or less doing the same thing on the same plane at the same time. Brass instruments are a little different, using only one hand to play the notes, but beware if you tell a French horn player that they play an easy instrument.

Chris continues to drill me on both the bowing technique and fingering. At the end of one lesson, there is my first epiphany, and the tone rings out true and resonant. But I am playing on open strings. When I add the left-hand fingering, the pitch goes off. I work on the pitch and get it to sound OK, but then the tone is off. I can pat my head and rub my belly, but not quite at the same time.

Nevertheless, she sees enough progress in six lessons to say that we are ready to pick an end piece. The way she reacts when I say I would like to play Max Bruch's mournful *Kol Nidre*, is a surprise and makes me realize that her attitude toward me is changing. The early Chris would have abruptly dismissed my hopeful idea with a brusque wave of the hand. Instead, she takes out her own cello, plays the opening phrases, and lets me see for myself how that piece is far beyond my ability, with fingerings in second and third position, way up toward the bridge.

By her warming up to me, and the nature of the whole project, I am now enjoying the lessons more. Chris knows that I want to play a serious piece of music, so instead of *Kol Nidre*, she suggests a Bach march in G major. My ego lights up at the idea of playing Bach but dims with the notion of a march. *A Bach march? What about a fugue, or toccata? Or a sonata or partita?* That's what you think of when you mention Bach. But a march?  Hordes of brass at half-time at a football game or patriotic Fourth of July parades are what come to mind when you think of a march. I start to question her choice, but her steely-eyed look tells me clearly that she is not yet all warm and fuzzy and that without her saying another word, I know I will be playing that Bach march.

Her victory over me on the choice of the final piece notwithstanding, Bach is not in her immediate plans for me, anyway. She is still a stickler on pitch, which, without frets on the fingerboard to guide me, continues to be my nemesis. It would be so much easier if the cello had frets, as on a guitar, banjo, or even a sitar. Each raised fret demarks a note, and you can feel where to put your fingers.  But no such luck on the cello.

For lack of frets, I fret.

Chris talks about building muscle memory for finger placement to get the pitch right, and the only way to get it is with repetition, repetition, repetition, repetition, repetition, and more repetition. Scales, and only scales, are her pre-scribed medication. Scales will try a man's patience in the best of circumstances, but in order to play in tune, I have to play them with excruciating slowness.

After several highly disciplined practice sessions with scales at home, there is a payoff. My pitch improves and holds when I take out the lesson book and do regular exercises.

While I practice the assignments for fingering and bow-ing, I can't resist the temptation and take out the Bach march and read it through. Not well, but well enough to get the gist of how it sounds. Even in an oom-pah 2/4 march rhythm, it sounds like, well, it sounds like Bach. I am happy.

I played a lot of sports in high school and even played college and semi-pro baseball. Now it's tennis, and I'm noticing a lot of similarities between sports and music. Both take commitment, discipline, focus, and an unusual combination of relaxation and intensity. When you try something new, it usually doesn't come to you right away. So it is with music lessons. I slog, and slog, and slog through mistake after mistake saying, "No, that's not it. No, that's not right. How am I supposed to do that again?"

More often than not, the more you push and try to bull your way through it, the worse it gets. Instead, you have to break things down into small components, be it two measures of music on the cello or just the overhead ball toss for a tennis serve. Then, step-by-step, you put the pieces back together and hopefully create something whole.

One day that is just what happens. I am relaxed; I look at the notes, start to play, and the music takes over. There is no separation of fingering and bowing, they are as one, and the sound is fluid, sonorous, and immensely gratifying. This is how a cello is supposed to sound, like the soothing voice of a father—strong, assured, and compassionate.

There were times as an athlete when I felt I was in "The Zone," and this is a lot like it but with an added dimension; it has soul. It is thrilling not to be fighting the instrument but to be at one with it.

Once you make a breakthrough, you hope that you can repeat it the next time you sit down to practice. More than likely, it doesn't happen that way. You revert, and it doesn't go as well as the last time. What you hope for is that the next good time *will* come, and it will come again. You cross your fingers that the intervals between the good sessions will get shorter until you can count on playing with decent technique every time you sit down and can then concentrate on the music.

During a practice breather at home, I realize that something is happening between the cello and me, and it's not all about music. I am beginning to have a relationship with it. I feel comfortable and at ease when I sit down with it, like sliding into a booth at a local breakfast place with a good friend, with a steaming cup of coffee poured even before you settle in. I don't really want to give it up, but the lessons are coming to an end.

I am not fatuously in love with the cello, and I have no Pygmalion fantasies that will land me on a friendly psychiatrist's couch, but there is a connection forming that I did not expect. To play the cello, you almost embrace it. It is, after all, between your legs, suggestive enough to raise that shrink's eyebrows. But it is your arms surrounding it and your hands that are almost, but not quite touching on the fingerboard that forms the bond.

To have the cello respond the way you want it to, you have to have the right touch; too gentle and it sounds bored, weak, listless, and watery; play it too roughly and it is scratchy and irritating. The cello is a knowing instrument. When you play it right, it reverberates with a rich, full-bodied, and satisfying hum.

The fact that it only rings true when you are on pitch and

bowing correctly is a testament to the luthier's art. All the elements that go into building a cello are in such perfect harmony that if even one is out of whack, it will never give you the sound you are listening for. It took centuries to perfect the shape and proportions of today's cello, but it has not been improved upon much since the 1700s.

Before then, the cello was larger and was played standing up. It had a softer sound than the modern cello because the strings were made from gut, just as they were for the early double basses. Some well-known names, all from northern Italy around the town of Cremona, made the best early cellos, Andrea Amati, Gasparo de Salò, and Giovanni Paulo Maggini among them. Amati built cellos for King Charles IX of France, and most cello music was written for royalty or the aristocracy to be played in somewhat intimate chamber settings.

Andrea Guarneri, another renowned name, was of the Venetian luthier school, and along with those in Cremona, needed skilled craftsmen. They attracted German luthiers from Füssen, the German instrument building hub, who were willing to migrate because the guild there had limited the number of luthiers to twenty, an early example of protectionist labor policy!

By the time Antonio Stradivari started building cellos, sometime after 1710, wire wound strings were in use, and his design became so popular that cellists had their older, larger cellos literally sawed up and reconfigured to the dimensions and proportions of the Stradivarius. It is that design that is basically today's cello.

There seems to be a difference of opinion as to when music was first composed expressly for the cello and who wrote it. It was either Giulio Arresti, as far back as 1665, or J.S. Bach, who composed his *Six Suites* for cello, beginning in 1717. By mid-century, Luigi Boccherini was composing and playing full cello concerti, and the instrument was taking its place along with the violin as a virtuoso string instrument.

After the French Revolution, performances became more democratic and were held in larger venues. The orchestras grew larger, and to meet the demands for increased volume, crispness, and a fuller, richer, more brilliant tone, the cello's bridge was raised so the strings could be tighter and project the sound more. The neck was set back at more of an angle, and the internal bass bar and sound post were reinforced to take on the additional pressure.

Although the cello looks uncomplicated, there are some seventy different parts in it, including the wonderfully medieval-sounding bouts and purflings, words conjuring up a castle siege.

Back in my high school days, I had a classmate, Ellen Carter, now Elena Delbanco, the daughter of Bernard Greenhouse, the late cellist of the Beaux Arts Trio. Greenhouse owned a Stradivarius cello, the Countess of Stanlein, as it is known, and I may even have seen it, although I doubt it, at Ellen's apartment one time or another. Of course, in those days, I would rather have held a Mickey Mantle Louisville Slugger than a Strad. But when Greenhouse died and his cello was sold at auction, the winning bid was expected to be between $5,000,000-$7,000,000. Even Mick's bat could not compete with that.

After her father's death, Elena wrote a novel about the Countess of Stanlein called "The Silver Swan." It's a good read.

It is the last day of my twelve cello lessons, and in a somewhat melancholy mood, I am playing the Bach *March in G* for a smiling Chris. It sounds better than when I played *The Ode to Joy* at the end of my bass lessons. Chris and I are sitting together at the end of the session, and she says, "I'm going to miss you. You have a certain knack for the cello." I am speechless. Chris has changed from a stern taskmaster to a companionable mentor, but she is not a flatterer. She means what she says. Hmmm. We look at each other. "What if...." I start to say, then leave the thought hanging. Chris picks up on my timid uncertainty. "What if you didn't stop? What if you move on to another instrument for the book but also continue with the cello?"

Is that madness? Two instruments at the same time? After all, I am not really a musician. Another "hmmm" moment. I am sitting with the cello nestling comfortably within the bower of my legs, my arm cozily slung around its shoulder. I cock my head to one side. I smile. And nod.

"I'd like that."

A pause.

"I'd like that, too," says Chris.

# The Viola

*Viola player wins Royal Opera House case for hearing damage. The Guardian, April 2018.*

*Mr. Christopher Goldscheider, from Biggleswade, Bedfordshire, a violist with the Royal Opera House orchestra, was seated directly in front of the brass section for a rehearsal of Wagner's thunderous opera Die Walküre, in the famous orchestra pit of the opera house, in Covent Garden. The bell of a trumpet was immediately behind his right ear during the rehearsal, and noise levels reached 132 decibels —roughly equivalent to that of a jet engine. BBC News, April 2018.*

This unfortunate incident may be the most attention a

viola player has ever had. Those who play the violin or flute, oboe or cello are the ones that customarily make the head-lines. They are used to being in the spotlight. But attracting attention is just not part of a viola player's DNA. They are a very unassuming, largely anonymous lot.

Even the instrument itself lacks a distinct identity. The viola does not have the petite refinement of the violin, the voluptuous curves of the cello, or the hulking mass of the double bass.

Looking like a hefty, somewhat swollen violin, the viola doesn't project sound as well as the other strings. It produces a softer, brooding, melancholy, and modest tone. It is the archetypical wallflower, barely seen and seldom heard. Yet the viola is an essential thread in the overall fabric of the orchestra, an intentionally internal voice. It functions as mortar does to brick. It holds the structure of the music together, providing a compositional harmonic interface between the higher and lower instruments.

I have tried during a concert to focus on listening only to the viola section, to single out their part in the music, and find it very difficult. I can tune my aural dial to the violins, cellos, basses, and any of the winds, and get clear reception. Their musical lines come through loud and clear. Try as I may though, my antennae cannot pick up the violas.

It would be interesting to attend an orchestra rehearsal where sections play separately before they are combined into the full ensemble in order to hear what a score sounds like without violas. I suspect they would be appreciated more in their absence than in their presence. It is like wearing underwear, which is an absolute essential, and you would never be caught without it, yet it goes unnoticed.

This extremely low-key reputation, to be so anonymous as to be almost invisible, is fine with most violists. At the risk of profiling them, they are typically very nice, calm, modest, and undemanding folk who seem to prefer cooperation to competition.

Just how anonymous are violists?

Consider this tongue-in-cheek tale. A symphony conductor is in frail health and so cannot go on a two-month tour with the orchestra. The principal viola, a fine musician, is asked to take his place on the podium. He does so and leads the orchestra through forty-five concerts on three continents in sixty days. After the tour, the regular conductor resumes his post, and the viola player takes his usual seat back in the viola section. As he does, his standmate leans over and says, "Hey, where you been?"

Most viola players take this kind of ribbing with a grain of salt. The truth is, they like being in the background. If they were pianists, they would be accompanists. It is uncertain how the relationship begins. Does being even-tempered, reliable, and not easily excited lead someone to the viola? Or does the viola have an innate attraction for that type of personality?

As modest as violists tend to be, they are fiercely defensive about their role in the orchestra, likening the viola to the drive shaft of a car. It is what meshes with the other parts, the engine and the transmission, and keeps the whole thing moving forward.

Some great composers played the viola, including Bach, Mozart, and Beethoven. I can imagine a young Mozart scampering through the palace, begging musicians to puh-leeze play the viola, and being snubbed by every wigged and long-stockinged violin player he could corner. Perhaps that's why he played the viola. Nobody else would. I can't quite see Bach or Beethoven behaving that way, but maybe they knew better and didn't even try.

The viola's blessing is also its curse. Its mellow, blending, middle voice is needed to smooth out rough edges in symphonic and chamber compositions, but for the same reason, it doesn't have star quality, and there is not a great abundance of solo viola music.

There are more than a smattering of pieces for solo viola, but nothing compared to the violin. The most well-known were written by Carl Stamitz, Ralph Vaughan Williams, Paul Hindemith, and Béla Bartók. But not many of us can hum a viola tune.

Many violists found their instrument through the back door. It was not their first choice. A common story is that in middle school, there were no more violins left when the student, perhaps late to class, came by to pick up their instrument. But there was a viola.

Even one of the lions of the solo viola, the Englishman Lionel Tertis, came to the instrument by accident. A violinist as a young man, one of his fellow students wanted him to join their string quartet, but they already had two violins and a cello. "You want to join? Grab that viola over there, and you're in."

Both Tertis and his Scottish colleague, William Primrose, did their best to popularize the viola in the 20th century, and amongst those who care, their names are legendary. It's just that not that many people seem to care, then or now. The audience is small, especially when compared to those who flock to hear a top violinist. Virtuosos like Itzhak Perlman, Joshua Bell, or Hilary Hahn can sell out Carnegie Hall or the Kennedy Center. Still, even free seats for a Yuri Bashmet or Tabea Zimmermann concert, two of the world's best violists, might go begging.

It is too bad, but not many of us have the opportunity to hear a solo viola performance. It is different from listening to the other solo strings. It has neither the brilliantly vibrant highs of the violin, the chesty resonance of the cello, nor the rumbling thunder of the double bass.

Because we hear the solo viola so rarely, it is a rich musical experience and worth seeking out. It has a honeyed tone, thick in a good way, and very personal. The sound flows around you like the current of moving water. It seems to be talking to your inner self, exploring musical nooks and crannies that other instruments leave untouched.

Its sonority and unobtrusive character notwithstanding, contemplating playing the viola scares me. Coming late to any kind of MI (Musical Intelligence), the viola's clef signature is confounding. Viola music is not written in either the treble clef or the bass clef. It has its own, the alto clef.

The signature looks like a baroque three or a gothic five with a Gambel quail's plume on top. The staff has the normal five lines, but middle C is on the middle line, not where it is in either the treble or bass clef.

The confusion is the piano's fault. The piano notation is drummed into us so deeply that we don't really stop to think that a C notation in the treble clef is not on the same line as a C in the bass clef. We are no more conscious of that anomaly than we are of writing the letter S differently in cursive than we do when we print it. We know it is the same letter even though it looks different. We become so hard-wired to bass and treble clef that a third clef, the viola's alto clef, feels like it is coming from outer space.

It is not just me who thinks it is difficult. Several viola primers use mnemonic devices to help students remember which notes are on which lines of music. For example, some suggest using Fat Alley Cats Eat Garbage as an aid. It means the staff lines are occupied by F-A-C-E and G. On the other hand, the spaces between the lines are occupied by G-B-D and F, or Grand Boats Drift Flamboyantly.

But those random phrases don't make any sense. They are meaningless and no easier to remember than learning the notes by rote.

I would prefer something like Fabulous Ace Cards Earn Gelt, and Good Boys Deserve Flannel. There is an aspirational element to those phrases that would surely spur students on to master the alto clef. Play your poker hand right, and you will win. And what youngster would not want a nice red and black plaid lumberjack flannel?

As if this weren't befuddling enough, when the music goes into the space above the staff lines, the legend, as it is called, the clef shifts from alto to treble. Yes, treble.

My brain must be less flexible than the average viola player, but to me, it would be like driving down the road in the U.S. one minute, then *poof!* All of a sudden, you are in England, and if you don't switch to the other side of the road very quickly, something nasty is likely to happen.

I look at some viola music, and I have to hesitate at every note to transpose whatever it looks like in treble or bass clef into what it is in alto clef. It is a job fit for a United Nations translator. Every other instrument is very content to say it is a member of the treble or bass clef family. But not the viola.

I also look at the full score of Beethoven's *String Quartet No.1* quite at random. I want to see if I can look at two parts written in treble clef for the violins, one in bass clef for the cello, and one in alto clef for the viola, and fathom how it will sound. For me, it's impossible. I can more or less follow one line, but then jumping to another line with a different instrument and a different clef leaves my head spinning.

It is as if I were in the middle of a good book, one I really like, and when I turn the page, suddenly the writing is in Arabic, Cyrillic, or Hebrew. I could not make heads or tails of it.

I have driven myself into a dither over the viola and am facing an existential question: to play or not to play. I like the viola. I like viola players. I am sure I can find a good viola teacher. But given how different it is from the other strings, can I expect to play something reasonably listenable on the viola in just twelve lessons?

I can hear my friends derisively clucking at me for being a chicken if I decide to avoid the viola and move on to the violin. I can also hear my future viola teacher saying after a few lessons that maybe this wasn't such a good idea after all.

Over the years, I have often advised people in a similar quandary to gather as much information and data as they can, give it serious thought, look at it from all sides, then come to a decision, but...don't act on it yet. After making the decision, take a pause. Do a gut check. How does the decision feel in your gut? If you feel fine, go with it. But if you get a funny feeling in your stomach thinking about what you have decided, back off. It's not the right one.

I follow my own advice. Maybe I am not mellow enough to do justice to the viola and the wonderful viola players who selflessly assure that the music we love is blanketed with their comforting inner voices. Maybe I am a chicken. Or maybe I know myself well enough not to push beyond my limitations. I make the decision to take a pass on the viola and hope that my gut check will not fail me. It is not quite as flimsy a decision-making process as waiting at a seance for the medium to connect with the spirit world for an answer, but it is a long way from a strictly rational analysis.

A day goes by, and I feel a sense of relief. The decision has passed the gut check, and instead of starting the search for a viola instructor, I pick up the phone and ask an orchestra friend of mine if she knows a good violin teacher.

Nobody questions my decision to avoid the viola, and that makes me a little sad. The viola doesn't have a lot of advocates or cheerleaders. The feeling is the same that I have for the kid who always gets chosen last for pick-up sports games, or the one who doesn't get asked to the Prom. It doesn't change my mind about playing the viola, but it makes me vow to be especially nice to the next viola player I meet.

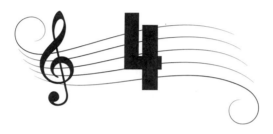

# The Violin

Perhaps more than any other orchestral instrument, the violin is the ultimate showpiece for virtuosity. The musical feats of legendary violin virtuosos, such as Niccolò Paganini, Fritz Kreisler, Jascha Heifetz, and Itzhak Perlman, are astounding. To see the score of a Paganini Caprice is a double wonder; how did a composer imagine such a torrent of notes, and how could a mere mortal actually play them with precision, tone, and emotion?

"He is gifted," people will say of a stellar violinist. "He's a natural," say others. "Well, he started when he was four!" exclaims a third as if that explained it all.

But with Perlman, for example, would his genius have

been lost had he not, just by chance, heard a violin concert on the radio when he was a mere three? What was it that so stirred that toddler that he knew right then and there that he wanted to play that instrument? He taught himself at first on a toy fiddle (being denied admission to a music conservatory because he was too small to hold a real violin) but was studying in earnest when he was still only five.

Had that serendipitous event not happened, might he have instead gone into the lingerie business on Seventh Avenue in New York and later retired to Florida to get a good Copper-tone tan and play gin rummy with other Sun Belt émigrés near the beach?

And if that radio broadcast had been a flute or oboe concerto, would he have been just as captivated and become just as great on either of those instruments? Or is there some-thing inevitable about genius finding its true path in life?

None of that speculation applies to me as I move on to the violin.

Parallels are not often drawn between the violin and the bagpipes, the one making angelic music that can bring tears to our eyes with emotions of love and longing, and the other, with its fortissimo-only boldness that can either bring tears to our eyes and expletives to our lips or stir the heart with strength and courage, even leading men into battle as late as the Second World War. The violin crumbles our defenses and finds resonance in the inner reaches of our souls. The bagpipes stiffen our resolve and prod us to dare to go where none have gone before.

But there is a parallel. It lies in how unmitigatedly awful

they each can sound in the hands of a beginner. I know that every master starts as a novice, but the sounds of a violin in the hands of a beginner are teeth-gratingly abominable, just like the bagpipes. They might do battle with each other to see which sounds most like a shrieking cat being twirled by its tail around the head of a sadistic madman.

Bagpipers have an excuse. The instrument is the devil to tune, especially in the days before plastic when the reeds really were made of natural cane from bamboo. Among the myriad, mostly bad, bagpipe jokes is the one that pipers spend half their time tuning and the other half playing out of tune.

To wit: A piper friend was hired to play at a Kirkin' O' the Tartan ceremony at a local church, a service to bless the tartan of a Scottish-American family. She arrived early and spent a solid half-hour laboriously coaxing her pipes into tune. She laid them down carefully on a desk in a basement classroom, shut the door firmly, and went to the restroom. Emerging much relieved, she was startled to hear someone blowing her pipes, horribly out of tune, and after all the effort she had gone through to put them to rights. Outraged, she stormed back to the classroom, flung open the door, and stood with hands on hips, ready to give the miscreant a thorough dressing down, only to discover her pipes untouched on the desk and the bagpipe-like sound coming from a vacuum cleaner being pushed around by the church custodian.

But a beginning violin player has no such excuse. The instrument is perfectly innocent. When it sounds bad, it is not the violin's fault. The failure to make it sound sweet and heavenly lies completely at the feet, or hands, of the player.

The violin is, so far at least, the only instrument that has prompted Doyen to ask with a polite, "If you don't mind," if I would close the door tightly before practicing. I cannot blame her. My early sessions are excruciating. It is not even remotely musical but does resemble the sound effects track of a screeching train, a door in badly in need of oil, and feedback from a faulty PA system.

It is too bad that it sounds so rough and scratchy in my hands so far because everything else about the violin is delicate and refined. The violin case is beautiful, with a hard, pebbled grain black on the outside and plush red velour inside to protect the instrument. But it is misleading in its elegance. There ought to be a warning label on it.

- Attention!
- Read carefully before using.
- Might cause animals and small children to flee and plants to shrivel up.
- Close all windows and doors before use.
- Prolonged exposure may lead to a stiff neck, deafness, and loss of friends.
- Not responsible for side effects, which may include ringing in the ears, grinding of teeth, sudden panic among housemates, prolonged isolation from human contact, and fantasies of ever playing anything remotely resembling music on this thing.

If there ever was a raw recruit for the violin, I am it. Nothing about the bass or cello has prepared me for this.

Even the basic posture is unnatural. Want to know what it feels like to hold a violin? Try walking around the house with an apple between your chin and collar bone for a while.

Nevertheless, as with almost anything we try that is new, even a dreadful beginning does not last forever, and with practice, what was at first awkward becomes more familiar and easier. In fact, much to my surprise, I am actually making progress faster than on the cello or bass.

It could be that since the violin is my third string instrument, if I had changed the order, whichever instrument was third would have been easier than the first two. I will never know the answer for sure, but I speculate that it has something to do with the higher pitch of the violin compared to the bass or cello. I seem to hear the notes clearly, and so I can stay in tune most of the time.

Playing off-pitch isn't ever good, but it is not so awfully bad if you are alone because even if you slide a little flat or a little sharp, you will still be in relative tune with yourself. But you cannot get away with that when playing in an ensemble, be it a duet, trio, quartet, or a larger group. When you are off, the entire harmonic balance is thrown out of kilter, and it simply sounds like a bunch of middle schoolers satisfying a music requirement.

That may be an obscure reference, but if you have ever been to a middle school concert, you know what I mean. Despite the misdirected plaudits of *Good job!* thrown at the young players by well-meaning friends and parents, it really wasn't a good job. It was barely tolerable. But woe to the person who doesn't smile bravely at the conclusion of the concert before scurrying home for a soothing, nerve-settling nightcap.

I've often thought that middle school music teachers have the patience of a saint. They are musicians, with a musician's ear, some with perfect pitch, who are nevertheless relentlessly, day after day, subjected to such an ear-splitting cacophony of un-musical sounds that it would drive an ordinary person crazy.

I have walked past a middle school music class and paused to try to figure out what instruments were in there. Some sounds were unrecognizable, yet these selfless teachers persist, and in many cases, introduce twelve- and thirteen-year-olds to a world of music that just might lay the groundwork for a lifetime of enjoyment.

Pricilla Arasaki, my violin teacher, is a Suzuki follower to the letter. The method is so prescribed that you can go from one Suzuki teacher to another, from New York to Stockholm, to Istanbul, to Bangkok, and if you are on page five of book two in one place, you can pick right up at the same point no matter where you are or who you have for a teacher.

The immutability of the method doesn't quite offend me, but the rigidity of it is contrary to my worldview, which tends strongly toward adaptability, alteration, and concessions to the individual.

With the Suzuki method, everyone is assigned the same tunes and plays them the same way. When you watch a group Suzuki recital, every violin is in exactly the same position under the jaw, and each bow stroke describes the same exact arc, as much mechanical as musical. It can get a bit monotonous playing *Twinkle-Twinkle Little Star* or *Go Tell Aunt Rhody* and other similar ditties over and over again, but there is a method to the madness. Each ear-worming tune has in it technical challenges that develop certain skills so you can move on from Book 1 to Book 2, then 3, and so forth, all the way up to Book 10. Some tunes help with string crossings, moving smoothly from one string to another, or slurring the notes in one upward or downward stroke of the bow, while others focus on tone, smoothness, staccato, and playing louder or softer.

There are some adult Suzuki students, like me, but the overwhelming majority are children, some as young as three years old. The method relies heavily on playing by ear and involves joint participation from a parent or other adult. The need to read music is minimized and put off until much later, sometimes only when the student wants to play in a school orchestra and realizes that reading music is absolutely essential.

Misgivings aside, I find it easier to play more fluently sooner with Suzuki, at least with the pieces that are in the curriculum. But it really is, and really does feel like a class and that I am in school again. When I look back at what I was playing at the same point in time on the bass or cello, the music was much more challenging. It seems as though the Suzuki method is especially good if you are in it for the long haul, and most Suzuki students are.

Despite the repetition, or as a Suzuki enthusiast would say, because of it, I am ready to consider the end piece. It is time to pick an excerpt from the classical repertoire and try to play it so that it is at least "reasonably listenable."

The literature is virtually unlimited. Everybody wrote for the violin, and the instrument seems to have been an instant hit with composers as soon as it sprang, seemingly fully formed, like Pegasus from the head of Medusa, in the middle 1500s.

Antecedents of the violin were from the Far East, but there is a huge leap from the bowed Chinese erhu or Arab rabab to the European violin. The violin's direct antecedent, the viol, looked somewhat similar and came almost a century earlier, but it was larger. You could not hold it under your chin. It was pitched much lower, had five to seven strings, and was tuned in fourths, like the bass, not fifths, like the violin. It also had a fretted fingerboard, unlike the violin.

So how did the violin burst on the scene from the workshop of Andreas Amati around 1550? It was not magic, but the evolution happened very quickly. A mere twenty years passed between the first documented appearance of a violin, albeit one with only three strings, in a painting by Guadenzio Ferrari in 1530 and the first attributable violin made by the aforementioned Andrea Amati in Cremona, Italy, in 1550. Who made the violin in the painting is still unknown, but accounts of the sound during those gap years talk about a softer tone and, yes, drone strings, just like drones on the unalterable bagpipes.

Although Amati is credited with having made the first violin, others appeared so close on his heels that it is likely that other renowned Italian luthiers, craftsmen such as Guarneri, Ruggiero, Stradivari, and da Salò, were making instruments of similar quality almost simultaneously. Like Jonas Salk and Albert Sabin working on a vaccine for polio at the same time in the mid-1950s, or Charles Darwin and Alfred Russell Wallace coming up with the theory of natural selection independently in 1858, this kind of world-changing, coincidental breakthrough is far from rare.

It must have been a frenzied and exciting time in Cremona and its environs as the luthier families vied with each other to lay claim to the prized forests in Lombardy to harvest the spruce and maple trees needed for their violins.

It may not be a stretch of the imagination to picture one of the Amati sons at the end of the day in his father's workshop, trudging down a cobblestone street to stop in at a local taverna to slake his thirst. Spotting a fellow luthier from the house of Stradivari, he invites the fellow to join him for a drink. In a dark corner, they find a thick, wooden table and pull up a couple of three-legged stools. The Amati orders leather flagons of wine, and with elbows on the tabletop, they talk about everything except what they really want to know. Both feigning affability and innocence, each one is trying to wheedle out of the other information on the secret details of how they make their violins. The Stradivari orders a second round, and in faux-loving fellowship, the Amati shouts for a third.

Rumor has it that a new Stradivarius has a superior sound, and Amati would love to know what slight adjustments his rival has made to achieve it. It could be the height of the bridge or the length and angle of the neck. Perhaps they have changed the depth of the bouts, the position of the sound post, or the chemistry of the varnish. Yes, it might be the varnish. These are the trade secrets that Stradivari might let slip, especially with another mug or two of wine. And so it could have gone. It is not hard to see that corporate espionage has deep roots and has not essentially changed very much over the centuries.

With all this history buzzing around in my head, I sit down to think about my end piece and conjure up images of sculpted busts of the great composers. Here is the scowling Beethoven, there the youthful Mozart, and Papa Haydn with his powdered wig. The pen I pick up is, in my mind's eye, transformed into a feathered quill, and as I dip its point into the imaginary ink well on my desk and write slowly, it practically sends shivers down my spine. Seeing the names appear at the tip of my pen, my quill, letter by letter, is an emotional connection to the flesh and blood person.

B-A-C-H.

B-R-A-H-M-S.

And for some reason especially,

S-A-I-N-T - S-A-Ë-N-S.

The letters flow together as I write his name as if they were music itself. It feels like he is moving my hand as I write his name. I dream one night, in a wonderful mixed metaphor that is only allowed in the world of dreams, that I'm watching Camille Saint-Saëns himself as he autographs a clean, white baseball with its raised red seams that I hold in my hand, standing along the third base line of a Los Angeles Dodgers' home game.

Ultimately, I decide, not on Saint-Saëns but on the Bach

*Air on a G string*, the arched eyebrows of my teacher notwithstanding.

The violin and I have made our peace, and I am making music. Doyen even told me that I don't have to close the door anymore. It gets to be the day before my eleventh lesson. I am playing the Bach *Air* pretty smoothly, and it is just a smidge away from being at least "reasonably listenable" and maybe even better than that. I am eager to play for my teacher to show her the marked progress from the previous week's lesson.

But the vagaries of thinking you know something when you really don't strike me hard. The lesson is a disaster. I play wrong notes, am out of tune, and screech and scratch with the bow like a parody of a violin student. Victor Borge, or Peter Schickele as PDQ Bach, would have had a field day with me. "Someone, please feed the cat," might be a wry Borge remark, while PDQ Bach could add: "Mmmn? When was that written? Ah yes, I see now, of course, it was written in a hurry, in broken thirds, in the key of B Very Flat Major Awfully Diminished."

I can't seem to get my left hand to recognize my right hand. They are like perfect strangers who are reluctant even to acknowledge the other's existence, much less be cordial or give a thought to working together cooperatively.

"What piece is it that you're playing?" Mr. Left would remark archly. "It's vaguely familiar."

"It's the same one you're supposed to be playing," would come the acid reply from Mr. Right.

Something inside me wants to play the *Air* really well,

not just "reasonably listenable," but smooth and even. I want it to conjure up the image of a punt, gracefully gliding across the surface of a still pond, with weeping willows along the shore dipping the tips of their feathery branches in the water, and pastel flowers dotting the mossy green banks. Perhaps my standard has gone up, and the level of proficiency that I achieved on the bass and cello is no longer good enough.

It is my subconscious at work, and I think it is influenced by a historical fiction book I just finished by the eminent psychiatrist Irvin Yalom. It is all about unconscious motivation and the angst that goes along with not being able to master it. In the book, it rules the two main characters, the philosopher Friedrich Neitzsche and Freud's early mentor Josef Breuer. In real life, they never actually met, but it is an engrossing story, and there is a lot of worrying in the book. I find that it's making me worry, too. I am worried about not being able to play the *Air* as well as I want to.

This is not what I planned. The whole idea was for this to be an adventure, an experiment of sorts, to see just what happens with each instrument. No outcome is preordained. "Que será, será." What will be, will be. It is to be a balance between the process and the results, but now the results are dominating my thoughts, and I wake up one morning calculating how many hours I can practice before my last lesson.

I am doing what my violin teacher told me to do, which is, after the requisite Suzuki Book 1 warm-ups, to play the *Air* at least ten times a day. But it is not helping. In fact, it is getting worse. I share this with Chris, my cello teacher (Remember, I liked the cello so much I decided to keep taking lessons). It is two days before the day of reckoning, and she says, "Stop playing altogether. Put away the violin. Don't play at all tomorrow, then play it through just a couple of times before your lesson."

"Are you serious?"

"Trust me," she says.

Uh-oh. Whenever I hear the words "trust me," it raises a red flag. It makes me feel a little leery about what might happen. Like the used car salesman who says, "Trust me, it runs like new," only to have the transmission drop out the next day. Or when the roofers' "trust me" has you skidding like an octopus all over the house with pails to catch the leaks the first time it rains.

Personally, I stopped using "trust me" thirty-seven years ago on a vacation in Hawaii with Doyen. We chose the former leper colony island of Molokai because it was less touristy than Maui, Kauai, or the Big Island, and while the leper colony is still there as a historic site, it closed as a leper center in 1969. The lure of a very beautiful, small island with only one resort hotel was irresistible.

One day we discovered an isolated crescent-shaped lagoon lined with leaning palm trees, explosively colored exotic flowers, and hanging vines. We swam lazily in the warm water of our private beach paradise until the sun started to go down.

Scantily clad as we both were, we almost felt like Adam and Eve, but with no apple tree in sight, we decided against that pretense. Instead, inspired by the steamy foliage, we channeled Tarzan and Jane, when lo and behold, just ahead on the path we were on was a dangling vine.

"Doyen," I enthused, "grab that vine and swing across that puddle while I take your picture."

"Are you sure it will hold me"

"Trust me," I said.

We are still married, but that was the last time I used that phrase.

I don't have much time to dither over whether or not to trust Chris and take her advice, but my playing does not improve, so I put the violin away and try not to think about it for what feels like a very long day without practice.

I slept well that night and spent the pre-lesson time the next day playing tennis, reading, taking a nice long walk with Doyen, and just casually playing through the *Air* a couple of times. I was pretending that how it sounded really meant nothing to me, something like whistling in the dark to scare away the ghosts and goblins.

At the lesson, which to me and my high expectations practically felt like an audition, I play the *Air* as well as I ever have. It is certainly "reasonably listenable" and maybe a notch above.

I think of what Chris told me and realize that trust is a profoundly deep belief in life, and that it is important not to reject "trust me" out of hand without considering the source. When warranted, the value of trust is inestimable. Trust me.

# First Interlude

The phone rang one evening, and it was my terrific older brother, Jerry. Jerry is retired now after an illustrious career in international investments. He was one of the good guys, watching carefully over the investments of thousands upon thousands of people in their state-sponsored pension plans.

He has the perfect resume with a baker's dozen of letters after his name: a BA from Yale (*magna cum laude* no less), LLB and MDiv from Harvard, and a DDiv from the Episcopal Divinity School. Doctor Mitchell, if you please.

He is a patron of the Charleston Symphony in South Carolina, and won something at a fundraising auction that he just had to tell me about.

I thought it might be a metronome, maybe a baton, or a history of music, but it was something quite different. It was an instrument.

"Wonderful!" I exclaimed, while at the same time wondering what he could possibly play, his musical ability having been abruptly cut short early in life by a total lack of rhythm matched by an uncanny inability to play or sing anything on key.

"Tell me more," I cautiously ventured.

"They're going to play Leroy Anderson's 'Sleigh Ride' at the Christmas concert, and I won the slapstick, you know, the thing that sounds like a whip."

"You won the slapstick?"

"I won the slapstick."

"What will you do with the slap stick?"

"Play it."

"Play it?"

"With the symphony."

"Play the slapstick with the symphony?"

"Yes."

"You?"

"Well, maybe not."

And here is where it got interesting. He went on to say that with my book about playing the instruments in the orchestra, wouldn't this be a splendid opportunity for me to actually perform one of them?

"Me?"

"You."

"The slapstick?"

"Yes."

I had already eschewed the entire percussion section and a lot more enticing instruments than the dubious slapstick, but I was nevertheless intrigued.

"OK, why not."

And that's when it got complicated. All was going well until the conductor of the Charleston Symphony told Jerry that there would be four rehearsals. I live in Colorado, and that's a lot of toing and froing just for a chance to whack a slapstick seven times, which is what the music calls for.

Jerry tried to persuade me to do it, but the more he talked about how much fun it would be, the more I realized that really, in his heart of hearts, what he wanted was to do it himself. I said as much, and after only a modicum of hemming and hawing, he agreed and somewhat sheepishly said, "Actually, I've already watched how to play it on YouTube, and I think I can do it."

After the concert, he told me that he nailed six out of the seven slaps.

# The Clarinet

Pre-adolescence is such a strange time in life. You are no longer a child, past those years when everything was generally straightforward and simple. Back then, your world was compact; you knew who you were, and were pretty clear about your relationships with family and friends. It is why we so cherish our childhood years. Life had not yet become complicated or conflicted. But as you enter puberty, you are transitioning to something...else.

If you are lucky, the certainty of childhood gives way to wide-eyed wonder about the endless possibilities of your expanding world. But more than likely, it effervesces into bobble-headed confusion and unanswerable questions.

Changes confront you daily. Changes in your body and in your mind seem to happen to you without you willing them or wanting them, much less understanding them.

Leading the way in this giant step into the world of puberty is gender differentiation. There was a time when there were just some things that boys did and some that girls did. Not so much now, but that was certainly the case when I was growing up. Only boys played baseball, and only girls played volleyball. Boys signed up for woodshop, and girls made jewelry. This kind of division is the only reason I can think of as to why I played the clarinet and not the flute. Boys took clarinet lessons. Girls took flute lessons. That's just the way it was at my school.

Fortunately, those turbulent years, while seeming to last forever when you are going through them, end up in the rearview mirror of your life and give you more than a few headshaking chuckles when you think back on them.

While music may have been an arbitrary gender separator back in middle school, it was a gender Mixmaster set on high in my adult life. Playing music heightens your emotional receptors and can connect you in a unique and intimate way with someone you are playing with. Although it was not intentional, twice when I sought out people to play chamber music with, much later and years apart, the flutist was a woman, and each time the mutual attraction went a little beyond Beethoven and Brahms.

That is not the only reason I am glad I took the clarinet. As much as I may have enjoyed the playing around as well as the playing, it was never a very important part of my life or major interest. Even dusting it off from time to time and playing again, it was always as a dilettante.

What I found out each time I tried it as an adult though, is that what you learn early in life, you never totally forget. It is like the old adage about riding a bicycle: no matter how many years have passed, when you pick up a bike again, you just get on it and go.

It can be good, like with a bike, but it can also be not so helpful. For example, playing a lot of baseball as a kid, in college, and one season of semi-pro ball, has kept me from being anything but a mediocre tennis player as an adult. I played so much baseball that I cannot unlearn the muscle memory of starting with your hands high with the bat and coming down to meet the ball in the strike zone. It is great for a baseball swing but not so good for tennis. A good tennis stroke starts with the racket head and hands low, hitting the ball in the equivalent of the strike zone and finishing high. Low to high for tennis, high to low for baseball.

The positive side of this latent muscle memory is serving me well as I reacquaint myself with the single-reed clarinet.

I still have the same clarinet I had in middle school, the one my malaprop-prone father called the "clariphone," probably mixing up the clarinet with Claribel, the clown from the Howdy Doody Show, and a saxophone.

It needed some work, and I was lucky enough to find a certified woodwind technician in our town who did a marvelous job reconditioning it. The always thin, wheezy B flat now was clear as a bell, and all the keys responded crisply and with less effort.

A few practice scales and I say to myself, "Holy mackerel, I can still play this thing!" Yes, I really do say "Holy mackerel" when pleasantly surprised.

I reach under the bed in the guest bedroom where my old études and scales books have been kept in a box for the last thirty-nine years and ever so gently lift them out and blow off the dust. The pages are browned like a piece of fried naan but flaky, more like a matzoh.

In an excited state of being, I whip through several exercises with relative ease, even some that I remembered having given me fits in the past. Has maturity given me a better understanding of phrasing, even as digital dexterity may have faded just a bit? The high notes ring, and the low notes have that wonderful, haunting, hollow sound.

This continues for a couple of days until I make a radical decision. I am not going to take lessons. I am going to go this alone. I can reach the goal of playing something from the classical literature so that it is "reasonably listenable" without a teacher. Or at least I think I can. And since I am not starting from scratch, as with the other instruments, I can do it in less time.

I do not think I am fooling myself because as I listen to myself on the clarinet, it is already way beyond the level I reached on the bass, cello, and violin. Practicing those other instruments, I could concentrate on either fingering or tone, but not both at the same time. Only toward the end was I able to put the two together. With the clarinet, I am playing that way almost immediately, and it feels very satisfying.

With the decision made to skip lessons and buoyed by my

continuing progress, I turn my attention to the end piece. What will I strive to play on the clarinet?

I am a sucker for schmaltzy, sentimental music, and having played Bach and Beethoven already, decidedly neither schmaltzy nor sentimental, I want something, if not schmaltzy, at least unabashedly heartfelt and melodic.

The nineteenth century was filled with composers who were masters of melody, and Schubert was one of the giants of the period. He did not compose much for solo clarinet, but he wrote beautiful parts for it in his chamber works, including the relentlessly beautiful wind octet. Sadly, all of those pieces are beyond this dilettante's ability.

Some of his piano pieces, however, have been transcribed for the clarinet and should be doable. YouTube is a wonderful source for listening to classical music performances by the greatest musicians of our, and even past, time, so I plant myself in front of the computer screen and start searching and listening.

I select Schubert's *Minuet in A major* and start to work on it, breaking it down into sections and then phrases of sections, and then even measures within those phrases. It's an approach that Chris Abbot, my cello teacher, taught me, and I understand how it works because of its similarity to mastering a skill in sports. A beautifully fluid tennis stroke starts with footwork, then a shoulder turn, racket preparation, racket speed, balance, eyes on the ball, forward movement, and follow-through.

Inevitably, I run into a troublesome phrase and log onto YouTube again to hear how it is supposed to sound.

In looking for the Schubert, I stumble onto the Adagio from Mozart's *Clarinet Concerto*. I listen to it once, then again, then once more, almost not believing how soulful it is. *Why didn't I think of it before?* It takes no more than a keystroke to switch away from Schubert and latch on to Mozart. Since I am already online anyway, I order the sheet music and have it to work on a couple of days later.

I know I can't play the fast passages in the Adagio at full speed, but I can play the slower parts. It is a little corny, but it feels like I am pouring how I live my life into this Adagio. It is a life filled with fresh challenges met with optimism, determination, compassion, and mostly good judgment. All life's normal emotional ups and downs, its joys and sorrows, seem to flow through the notes as I modulate the phrases and make music. It is feeding my soul, and I play it over and over and over again.

After playing, I feel so at peace. I wonder where else but in music can you find that same sense of inner harmony?

Mozart died two months after finishing the clarinet concerto and never heard it performed. He might not have recognized the way it sounds today because the first part was originally written for the basset horn. He abandoned it, then resurrected it for the basset clarinet, a now mostly ignored instrument that has a lower range than the modern B-flat clarinet. The instrument itself was invented in 1788 and was championed by Anton Stadler, a friend (and frequent jewelry and cash "borrower") of Mozart's, and the same person for whom he wrote his *Clarinet Quintet*.

Nobody can be certain when Mozart first heard the basset

clarinet, but given that Mozart, Stadler, and the instrument's inventor, Theodor Lutz, were members of the same Masonic Lodge and hung out together, he could have been among the first. Perhaps Lutz told his friends about the new instrument he was working on, and when Mozart heard it, it rekindled the old idea. Mightn't he have taken that put aside sketch for the basset horn and continued to work on it with the newer basset clarinet in mind? The result is what we now know as the *Clarinet Concerto in A Major*, completed in 1791.

Sinking into my chair after playing the Mozart one last time, I am done with the clarinet in a month instead of the usual three. Having a taste of what it is like to play an instrument better than "reasonably listenable," I momentarily wonder if I should abandon the project altogether and try to get really good on the clarinet. But the moment passes, and the lure of learning to play the rest of the instruments waiting for me is irresistible.

With a sigh and a certain degree of melancholy, I pack up my clarinet and box of sheet music and push them back under the bed in the guest bedroom.

# The Oboe

I remember reading in the *New York Times* some time ago that several of the major orchestras in the USA were looking to fill vacancies for their principal oboist at the same time. It was tantamount to an orchestral tsunami, the oboe being one of the key instruments that bestows upon an orchestra its signature sound. And to make matters worse, there were far fewer qualified oboists from which to choose to replace the retirees. Oboists are outnumbered by violinists, cellists, trumpeters, horn players, and clarinetists by a magnitude of almost geometric proportions.

In rapid succession, notices were posted that the principal oboist was retiring from no less prestigious orchestras than the New York Philharmonic, the Chicago Symphony, the Cleveland Orchestra, and the Los Angeles Philharmonic. Those were just the headliners. There were others.

What was happening? It could not possibly be a coincidence. There had to be some underlying cause for these stellar musicians to be retiring all at once. It was as if The Mob had infiltrated the oboe world. They had their own oboists you see, the sons of Dons who had paid good money to make sure their boys were legit. In city after city, the Bosses' Consigliere took the sitting principal oboist out to a nice lunch at a neighborhood trattoria. They sat him down at a plush banquette at the back of the restaurant, nice and private, and over a glass of vino rosso and a house special risotto, they "suggested" that it might be a good time for him to retire.

Of course, that is far-fetched, but this was really extraordinary. It was as if every all-star shortstop on four of the best teams in baseball all decided to quit at the same time. In this case, it was a generation of oboists packing up their reeds and calling it quits. I had to find out what was going on.

So, with one eyebrow raised and a twirl of my imaginary Hercule Poirot waxed moustache, I started to do a little detective work. All four of the departing principals from the majors were about the same age, most in their 60s, and most had been in their positions for between twenty and thirty years. Checking on their backgrounds, I discovered that three of them, plus five others who would retire soon or were considering retirement, had studied at the Curtis Institute of Music in Philadelphia. In the words of Lewis Carroll, this was getting "curiouser and curiouser."

Now channeling the resident sleuth of 221B Baker Street in well-tailored tweeds and with smoke from his calabash pipe curling into the shadows above his head, I deduced that there must be a common thread that tied all these top-flight musicians together.

What could it be? It turns out that the "what" was a "who." Flashback to France, April 1905. A young French oboist named Marcel Tabuteau auditions in Paris for Walter Damrosch, conductor of the New York Symphony. Tabuteau, just nine months removed from his graduation from the Paris Conservatoire, is extraordinary and is hired. He joins the orchestra in New York for the start of the 1905 season.

But all is not well in the Big Apple, where labor unions flex their muscles even in the rarefied air of the classical music world. The musicians' union objects to a French oboe player taking a job away from an American musician, and he is deported. He finishes his military obligation in France and then makes his way back to the USA in 1907. The union again cries foul, but this time it is unsuccessful in its strong-arm tactics, and Tabuteau is allowed to stay.

The man wastes no time, and his talent shines brightly. For the start of the 1908 season, he is named Principal Oboe with the Metropolitan Opera Orchestra. Tabuteau decides America is for him and becomes a citizen in 1912.

Just three years later, a blink of an eye in the often career-long tenures of orchestra musicians, he is on the move again, ever upward.

This time he becomes the Principal Oboe of the world-renowned Philadelphia Orchestra under Leopold Stokowski (and later another giant, Eugene Ormandy). He has found a home and will remain Principal Oboe for thirty-nine years, from 1915 until his retirement in 1954.

While he is securing and furthering his position and reputation as a performer, he is also developing a new system for teaching and playing the oboe at the Curtis Institute of Music in Philadelphia. The result is a new sound. It is not as he was taught in France, at the feet of his mentor, Georges Gillet, a master of the light, delicate, fluid French oboe—the aural equivalent of a tantalizing soufflé, and far from the throaty, thick, heavy, sauerkraut and hasenpfeffer sound favored by the Germans. Tabuteau's oboe is something different. It is neither the brittle, dried toast of the English oboists nor the antipasto vocalise of the Italians. It is a uniquely American sound.

Tabuteau has developed a creamy, warm, rich, more open, and expressive tone that adds depth and emotional color to the music in ways the European styles do not. What's more, he can teach it to others, along with the vitally important way to make the oboe reeds that help produce the American sound.

It is not that scores of accomplished oboists suddenly flocked to the Curtis Institute, but rather that he was able to take the raw students who came to him and mold them into startlingly good players.

This is where those now-retiring principal oboists all came from. Tabuteau's students were so successful that eleven of them came to occupy the first chairs of America's top symphony orchestras, including the Philadelphia Orchestra, The New York Philharmonic, the Boston Symphony, the Chicago Symphony, the Minneapolis Symphony, the Los Angeles Symphony, the National Symphony, and the NBC Symphony conducted by Arturo Toscanini.

Those principals taught the Tabuteau System to their students, some of whom also rose to the position of Principal Oboe in those and other orchestras.

It is little wonder that music critic Daniel J. Wakin succinctly summarized Tabuteau's influence in a 2005 article, almost forty years after Tabuteau died, by writing, "Through his teaching, he is universally credited with having created the American sound and style of playing the oboe."

The man was a legend of somewhat biblical fecundity who begat generations of superb players whose lineage, unto today, can be traced back to him. In fact, even I cling to that family tree. Tabuteau taught Robert Bloom, who taught Ray Still, who taught Peter Cooper, who is teaching me. I am afraid, however, the line will end there.

I am now studying with Peter, but he wasn't my first teacher. There aren't many oboe teachers in our area, so I signed on with the first one I found, and it came from a Google search. I usually say to myself and others, "Consider the source," when you get advice. For example, a recommendation for a must-see movie that turns out to be a dud. A to-die-for spaghetti carbonara that tastes more like mac and cheese. The sauce was as bad as the source. Or, fatally, the well-intentioned invitation to the "you'll-get-along-great" blind date that has you wishing you were a monk in a monastery. If you had only considered the source.

I should have taken my own advice. I don't personally know Mr. Google, and even though he certainly does have access to a lot of information, I don't always trust his judgment. I think he gets paid for some of the advice he gives.

As a result, I quickly realize that my googled teacher is a very busy woman with private students, a university adjunct professorship, who makes reeds, runs a cottage sewing business, has a husband, and, not least of all, looks after her two-year-old son.

The situation makes me feel like an afterthought, and when she goes off on vacation after only two lessons, I decide to at least explore the possibility of making a change. The search leads me to the University of Colorado Department of Music and the hope of getting a recommendation from someone there for another teacher. It turns out even better than I could ever have dreamed. By pure blind luck, I reach Peter Cooper on the phone and explain my project to him in my practiced thirty-second elevator speech so he doesn't hang up. He is actually intrigued by the idea and says he just happens to have an opening in his studio for the short term if I want to study with him personally. This is a Tabuteau acolyte and the Principal Oboe of the Colorado Symphony Orchestra, in addition to being a professor at CU. Without hesitation, I sign up for lessons and thank my lucky stars that the first go did not work out

It is not that my first teacher was bad, but after only one lesson with Peter, the contrasts are striking, showing that similar results can be achieved by vastly different approaches.

For example, you can get from France to England by ferry, train, or plane. Each one gets you to your destination, but not in the same way at all.

Imagine, if you will, a split screen with my first oboe teacher, whom we shall call Sarah, on the left, and my second teacher, Peter, on the right. Off camera, I ask both the same question. Now picture them answering my question simultaneously. It would sound like this:

Me:    How long should you soak the reed before playing?

Sarah: Four to five minutes

Peter:  About one minute

Me:    How much of the reed should you soak?

Sarah: Just the tip.

Peter:  The whole cane part, up to the winding.

Me:    How hard should you blow?

Sarah: It requires a lot of air, so take a deep breath from way down in your stomach and blow hard.

Peter:  Not very hard. Think of your breathing as soft but athletically ready in a state of infinite possibility.

Me:    What's the key to getting a good tone?

Sarah: Playing the low notes, especially the low D.

Peter:  Being able to play from C to C sharp just on the reed, before ever putting it in the oboe. Might take a week.

Not a lot of harmony in that duet.

Studying with Peter Cooper is uplifting. He is a raconteur par excellence, and his stories, though sometimes lengthy, do make a point that is helpful in learning the oboe. Many of them deal with the role of the subconscious in learning. He is not a new age guru or some ooie-ooie medium, but he firmly believes that a lot is going on in the learning process that we do not consciously control.

I am not ready to rely on my subconscious for anything yet and, in fact, find that practicing is taking on a different rhythm than with the other instruments. On the clarinet and strings, I could practice for a solid hour. But for the oboe, it's practice for fifteen minutes, put it down, read the latest news, or trim my toenails. Pick up the oboe again and practice for another ten minutes or so (the lips get tired more quickly the longer you play). Lay the oboe aside, change the water in the bird's cage, pick it up once more and practice until my lips are so tired that I dribble down my shirt front while taking a drink of water.

I can only go so far before my upper lip loses its grip on the double reed and flutters around, sounding like a whoopee cushion. My tired, flaccid lip flaps as loosely as the ears of a basset hound shaking its floppy ears after a bath.

The fatigue comes because the oboe embouchure is very different from the clarinet embouchure. The clarinet has a single reed attached to the mouthpiece with, essentially, a hose clamp. The oboe has a much smaller double reed, which is inserted into a small hole at the top of the oboe, the same way you would stick a candle into a candlestick.

The embouchure used on one instrument simply does not work on the other.

Embouchure. It is such a wonderful French word and so important. I should find out what it really means. Mumbling embouchure over and over to myself, emphasizing a different syllable each time, EMbouchure, emBOUchure, embou-CHURE, I get up from my desk to look for a French dictionary.

Saying embouchure out loud makes me chortle, remembering Steve Martin as the inept Inspector Clouseau trying to say "hamburger" in one of the Pink Panther movies.

I find many definitions for embouchure, most having nothing to do with musical instruments. For instance, some refer to embouchure as the mouth of a river, i.e., *Between Lake Tchitogama and the embouchure (mouth) of the Manouane River, the Péribonka is entirely navigable.*

For the insatiably curious and those who are guessing that Lake Tchitogama and the Manouane and Péribonka rivers are somewhere in what was once French West Africa, you are not even close. The Péribonka is about a three-hour drive north of Quebec City in Canada.

The most useful definition is simply that embouchure means mouth. As applied to musical wind instruments, it is interpreted as the way you form your mouth on your instrument.

Throughout my perhaps quixotic quest to play almost all the orchestral instruments, it is proving useful at concerts to follow an individual player more closely than I used to. Some oboists I see seem to be from the Sarah school in that they appear to be blowing their proverbial brains out, with red faces, lips pursed tightly in a death grip on the double reed, and eyes bulging, reflecting the back pressure Sarah had told me about. It would not surprise me if hospital ER rooms near music conservatories had oboe players with hernias and broken blood vessels as regular customers.

This technique doesn't seem healthy, and I wonder if that might also have contributed to all those Tabuteau descendants retiring at the same time. Can a lifetime of repeatedly blowing hard into a very narrow opening between two cane reeds be seriously bad for you? There is now incontrovertible evidence that many football players suffer concussions and even brain damage from repeated blows to the head, even though each one by itself is inconsequential. Maybe I should wear a helmet when I practice the oboe.

This also could just be an old wives' tale, an urban myth passed around to bolster the heroic stature of oboe players. I'll find out.

It does not take long for my research to turn up "Medical Issues in Playing the Oboe: A Literature Review," featuring no fewer than 950 separate studies of what happens to people who play the oboe.

Among the findings, I discover that "some evidence was found for musculoskeletal problems, focal dystonia, stress velopharyngeal incompetence, increased intraocular pressure and glaucoma, gastroesophageal reflux disease, lower pulmonary function, disease transmission via instruments, and hearing loss due to noise exposure."[1]

I understand the last two, but tremble at the thought of

being velopharyngeally impaired.

Peter has been very patient with me. His approach and my practice are developing a better embouchure and beginning to pay dividends. The steep learning curve is leveling out, and I can hear progress in my tone production, fingering, shifting octaves, breath control, and accuracy.

For my end piece, we pick the oboe solo in the final scene of Tchaikovsky's gorgeous music for the ballet *Swan Lake*. As we work on my technique, the ways Peter finds for me to overcome a technical problem are creative, spontaneous, and effective. If something doesn't work, he says, "OK, try this" until we find the solution. More than once, it is something he has never tried before, but it works. His innovative teaching is helping me to move on and grow.

In preparing the *Swan Lake* piece, I notice that my standards have changed since the start. What was "reasonably listenable" on the bass or violin now seems not good enough. The clarinet raised the stakes because I had played it before when I was young, and the result was more musical and satisfying. Now with the oboe, my expectations are higher. I want *Swan Lake* to be substantially more than reasonably listenable.

Peter seems to understand this and becomes like a coach preparing me for a solo performance. He takes my goal of Swan Lake seriously as if his reputation were at stake, and he had to have me ready at the end of the twelfth lesson to play that piece as well as an advanced student.

After learning the excerpt passably well technically, we talk about phrasing, dynamics, and emotion. With a bow to the subconscious, I paint a mental picture of how I want the music to sound.

*Softly, the graceful swan glides **pianissimo** effortlessly across the water of a pond, barely disturbing the smooth surface at first, then **mezzo-forte**; she spreads her wings as if stretching languidly after a restful sleep. She glides again with a touch more energy, leaving a perfect V in her wake. Then, stretching her neck and beating her wings in powerful strokes, she lifts from the water as the music rises to a **double forte** conclusion on a pair of insistent high C-sharps as the oboe is joined by the orchestra to celebrate the great bird's ascent.*

That is all well and good subconsciously, but I am not there yet empirically. What you *want* to do and what you *can* do are not always the same. As the great philosopher Yogi Berra once said, "In theory, there is no difference between theory and practice, but in practice, there is."

The biggest obstacle is practice itself. Like the lost New York tourist who sees an old violinist busking on the sidewalk with his case open for tips and asks him, "How do you get to Carnegie Hall?" and is told, "Practice, practice, practice."

The hardest part of practicing is the tedium, drudgery, discipline, and plain hard work day after day, between the exciting beginning and the hopefully triumphant end.

There are days when I just don't feel like practicing—the days when things aren't going right; days I would much rather be doing something else like reading, playing tennis, taking a walk, or riding my horse. Days when there are other things I have to do and the morning slips by, the afternoon vanishes as if it were never there, and then after dinner, I am tired and spectacularly unmotivated to practice.

It is really no different from anything else you are trying to learn, get better at, or master. It could be your job, a language, or, hardest of all, becoming a better spouse, parent, or friend. Is there anything more important than that? Yet how much time do we spend purposefully being an altogether better person?

*Does my playing a bunch of instruments make me a better person? What am I not doing when I am practicing and writing that I could be doing to make a difference to someone I care about? Or perhaps equally important, someone I don't know but in whose life I might be able to make a difference?* I don't know if even Yogi could answer those questions.

Peter is tweaking my playing now, preparing me for my final lesson, which I think in his mind is my recital. He has given me unwavering encouragement and support all along, and it has helped me over the humps. Yet, the fact that he had doubts is revealed when at my last lesson I finish playing the *Swan Lake* solo for him, and he says softly, "That was amazing. In twelve lessons?"

Leaving the oboe feels to me like the end of summer vacation when you are young. The transitory freedom from school, lessons, church, and household chores (to teach us to be responsible), are all suspended during those magical months of summer.

The friends you make are likewise uninhibitedly close. You share things with summer friends you would never admit to with classmates you are bound together with for the whole school year, and who might take advantage and call you out one day in a fit of pique. If there is romance involved, it is all-consuming and so emotionally intense that you are absolutely positive that no one in the history of the world has ever felt as you do. In heart-wrenching farewells, you swear you will stay in touch through the year, and at that moment, sincerely believe you will. But the falling leaves of autumn and the drifting snows of winter cover not only the frozen ground but also extinguish the burning passion that thrived in the heat of summer.

The twelve lessons on the oboe pass so quickly that I am not really prepared to move on, but like the calendar signaling the end of summer, I must. And as an adult, I know that although I may miss the oboe at first, I will relegate it to a fond corner of my private memories, just as I did with a long-ago summer romance. I will take the next step and look forward to the next adventure, challenge, joy, and discoveries that lie in wait, if not in ambush, as I continue to plow my way through the orchestra.

# The Bassoon

I have been looking forward to the bassoon and its rich, mellow, almost human timbre. In that sense, it is much like the cello, although the bassoon has a more avuncular quality. It is rounder, with more of a harrumph sound, like the uncles in Dylan Thomas's *A Child's Christmas in Wales*, whom he describes as "...large men (who)...sat in front of the fire, loosened all buttons, put their large moist hands over their watch chains, groaned a little and slept." Those uncles had a soothing and endearing presence, and so it is with the bassoon.

Yet as melodious as Dylan's words are, "All the Christmases roll down toward the two-tongued sea, like a cold and headlong moon bundling down to the sky that was our street," music itself is almost absent in his recollection. Not until near the very end does he find and remember, "Always on Christmas night there was music." As he readies his childhood self for bed, he writes that he could "... see the lights in the windows of all the other houses on our hill and hear the music rising from them up the long steadily falling night."

Dylan wrote those words in 1945, and now all these years later, another Christmas is approaching, and I recall my own connection to *A Child's Christmas in Wales*. It is of me at home with my family, sitting by the fire and reading Thomas's story to our kids, Ben and Liza, every Christmas Eve.

In stop-action photo memory, I see them flick from cross-legged pajama-snuggled bundles melting sleepily into Doyen's lap, to patiently listening to me as they played quietly together on the floor, to exchanging looks across the room as I turned the pages, to fondly remembering the early times themselves when coming home from college for Christmas.

Feeling pangs of nostalgia, I wonder if I can do something that might come close to recapturing the warmth of those days, even though Ben and Liza have grown up and live from middling-far to very far away.

Ben and Anna, his partner of sixteen years, live in Los Angeles and lead a very cool, socially hip, urban lifestyle filled with restaurants, shows, art, and business. Liza lives with her boyfriend Dan and two dogs in their house in the Colorado mountains, and their idea of a good time is to hike up to a 12,000' mountain peak in two feet of snow and ski down it.

Neither Ben nor Liza is married, but they have two of the best relationships I've ever seen: honest, loving, full of laughter, with mutual respect, trust, and compassion for others.

They have chosen not to marry, and although at first I was disappointed, I now not only accept their decision but also embrace it. So often, we decide not to choose some very important things in our life. For example, how many people actually choose a religion?

Most are born into one and are told by their parents that that's what they are, and so, that's what they are. Likewise with marriage. It seems that so many couples just bind themselves together because that's what comes next in life, or like high school seniors who, without a second thought, trundle off to university the following year. It's just what you do. Might not we all be better off if we stopped first and thought more purposefully about our choices for these and other fundamental and foundational decisions in our lives?

Whatever others think, I have respect for our kids' choices and an overflowing barrel of love to go along with it. That is why I want to put some emotion into this Christmas, especially since circumstances dictate that we will not all be together.

Even though I've only taken four bassoon lessons and Christmas is next week, I decide to try to learn something Christmassy, video it, and send it as a surprise to Ben and Liza on Christmas Eve. The caroling boys in *A Child's Christmas in Wales* debated between *Hark the Herald* and *Good King Wenceslas*, but I pick *Silent Night*, the carol I used to sing Liza to sleep with almost every night when she was a child, even in July. It was soothing for her, a gentle sliding into a silky, settled, and sound sleep.

I practice hard for the few days that are left before the big night, and I think I am ready. Doyen is the videographer, equipped with a steady hand and a five-year-old iPhone. We light a fire in the same fireplace as in the old days, using logs of fragrant pine and the hotter, slower-burning black walnut from a diseased tree we had to take down. It is ablaze, and we dim the lights so that the mood is set by the firelight. I arrange myself and the bassoon on a nicked and gouged bow-back chair, and in the surrounding quiet, broken only by the occasional click of the settling logs, I play *Silent Night*. Only I flub some notes, and so I have to do it again. And again. And again. I make it through the next time, all except for the second to last note. "Once more unto the breach, dear friends, once more," quoth I.

Had I been Henry V at Agincourt, the English would have lost, and we might now all be speaking French. Once more would not have been enough to prevail. But I persevere, and after a few more takes, few in this case meaning twelve, we get one that is good, and off it goes sailing through the ether to far-flung Los Angeles and the Colorado mountains.

Along with the video goes this, which is much more an homage to John Betjeman or Ogden Nash than to Dylan Thomas:

*'Twas the week before Christmas,*
*It was coming so soon,*
*And with only four lessons*
*On my rental bassoon*

*I'd little time*
*To sound like it oughta*
*A Christmas gift*
*For my son and my daughter.*

*I imagined myself*
*In a fireside scene,*
*Playing a carol*
*Soft and serene.*

*So I practiced hard*
*To get the right sound*
*But it came out too throaty*
*Not subtle and round.*

*Then angels descending*
*From afar did come*
*To see what in*
*The hell I had done.*

*What's that noise?*
*Let's make it cease!*
*It's Christmas, you know,*
*A time of peace.*

*I pleaded with them*
*(I'd now less than a week)*
*How to get rid of*
*That high B flat squeak.*

*That's not so hard,*
*Quite easy, you see,*
*Just give a quick flick*
*On the thumb B flat key.*

*Lo and behold!*
*It worked just like magic*
*Without their advice*
*It would have been tragic.*

*So I put behind worry,*
*And put behind fright*
*And played straight through*
*To the end, Silent Night.*

I cannot help myself being amazed every time I start a
new instrument. It could be similar to what Darwin might
have felt when he came across a new creature that he had
never seen before. *What exactly is this thing? What is it
related to? How did it come to evolve? Where does it fit into
the larger scheme of things?*

Predecessors of the modern bassoon date back to the 16th
century. Rackett, Shawm, and Dulcian, despite reading like
names on a plaque of a law firm, were actually early iterations

of the bassoon. To allow composers to score lower notes, variants were made bigger and bigger until one version measured almost nine feet long. As you can imagine, it was very difficult to handle and play and looked like a close cousin of the Swiss alphorn or Australian didgeridoo. An inventive dulcian maker solved the problem to some extent by making a U-turn with the long, straight tube, which effectively halved its size. Now players could transport their instrument without borrowing their father-in-law's ox cart.

These somewhat primitive instruments served composers well as a bass continuo foundation in compositions, often merely doubling the cello or oboe parts but an octave lower. One big problem, though, was that someone forgot about a couple of notes. The dulcian, for example, could not play two tones in a chromatic scale. It didn't have a low B or C sharp. Therefore, it could not play a lot of music. It would be like trying to do math but not having the number 5 or number 7. Adding 2+4+5+7 to get 18 could instead look like 2+4+8-3+(4x6)-20+3=18. It was a bit awkward.

Even with these shortcomings, and only four keys, the bassoon began to emerge from its relative orchestral obscurity when Bach, and especially Vivaldi, who wrote over thirty concerti for the bassoon, began to treat it more prominently.

Unlike other woodwinds that reached technical maturity rather quickly, the bassoon was a late bloomer, with ateliers and workshops continuing to tinker and improve its range, pitch, and sonority well into the 19th century. The Almanräder-Heckel workshop in Cologne, Germany, eventually developed a twenty-five-key bassoon, much like the ones played today. Except by the French.

The French, characteristically, did not particularly care for the German Heckel sound and so went a separate way. Just as Robert Frost wrote that "Two roads diverged in a wood, and I, I took the one less traveled by," so, too, did the French leave the main road to develop the Buffet-style bassoon on their own. Not many followed in their footsteps because the Buffet is not as bright and doesn't project as well in a large orchestra. Yet, its moody, introspective voice and dulcet tones in the higher register were well suited to the misty, impressionist compositions of Debussy and Ravel. Today, Buffet bassoons are rarely heard outside of France and Belgium.

My bassoon is in the Heckel style, though not a genuine Heckel. The cost of a brand-new Heckel is in the $50,000 range, and you might have to wait eight years to get one. But that doesn't lessen my excitement when the brown-clad UPS driver delivers, with signature required, my rental bassoon.

Opening the case gives me a bit of a fright, the same kind of exaggerated, melodramatic reaction that silent film's Margaret Dumont might have expressed on seeing Groucho Marx lurking behind a mirror in her boudoir. Perhaps startled would be a more accurate way to describe the sensation as I stare at what appears to be the dismembered trunk of a baby elephant lying before me in its velour-lined casket.

It is much, much bigger up close than it appears to be on stage in the orchestra, where it is often partially hidden behind a row of other woodwinds, with only its round chimney sticking up behind the ears of the clarinetists.

There are a few days before my first lesson, and I feel that I have to at least learn how to assemble and hold the bassoon beforehand. With five separate parts, the long joint, wing joint, butt, bell, and bocal, it looks complicated. I certainly don't want to put a square peg in a round hole, literally or figuratively, and ruin the instrument before I even put reed to lips. I need a tutorial, and what better place to find one than on YouTube, that know-it-all.

I expect to find one video or two, but YouTube has twenty-five on how to assemble and hold a bassoon. That is eight more videos than on how to change a cloth diaper, proof that it would, indeed, be difficult.

I need not have worried, as the videos are clear. Soon the bassoon is stretched out on the couch, fully assembled, although the way it doubles back on itself in a U-turn distantly resembles the P-trap under my kitchen sink.

There is a regular array of keys on the front of the instrument, not that different from the clarinet or oboe, but then on the back, hidden from view, are more keys. There are five for the left thumb and four for the right thumb. If my math is correct, that is nine keys for only two thumbs. This instrument clearly is made for people under forty who can thumb text with lightning speed on tiny screens while talking on the phone and watching a sit-com rerun at the same time.

I do not understand why it is so complicated, but I assure myself that this mystery will be solved once I start my lessons.

I do worry, though, about how to pick it up and carry it without breaking something since almost every inch of the

4'5" long instrument is covered with keys, holes, pads, and levers. What I feel is similar to the apprehension of a new father as he reaches for the first time for his delicate newborn son or daughter. Where exactly do I put my hands, and how am I supposed to hold it without dropping it on the floor?

Maybe this isn't really a bassoon. Someone is playing a practical joke on me, and the real one will come tomorrow. After all, the bassoon is often referred to as the clown of the orchestra, mostly by other musicians who playfully call it the farting bedpost. I find that bassoonists are the butt of almost as many jokes as banjo players, accordionists, and bagpipers, who all actually seem to revel in their outlier status.

Do you know what a bassoon and a lawsuit have in common? Everyone is relieved when the case is closed. Or that the definition of an optimist is a bassoonist with a 30-year mortgage. And finally, a bassoonist meets a friend and asks, "Did you hear my last concert?" to which the friend replies, "I certainly hope so!"

But jokes aside, the bassoon is a beautiful instrument, with its four-octave range and ability to evoke emotions from mournful longing to rapturous joy, giving it a versatility hard for other woodwinds to match.

After the petite, delicate, and temperamental oboe reed that you envelop with your embouchure, the bassoon reed feels like a doctor's tongue depressor. It is easily twice as wide, longer, and twice as thick. It is, however, a work of art; the double cane reed is intricately wound with multi-color threads, copper wire, and topped at the open end with a turban-like bulb.

In a departure from the pattern of the previous teachers, my current mentor, Roger Soren, and I discuss what the end piece will be after only a few lessons. I take this as a compliment and am enjoying my progress.

The iconic bassoon part representing the grandfather in Prokofiev's *Peter and the Wolf* is one option, as are excerpts from Ravel's *Bolero* and Rimsky-Korsakov's *Scheherazade*. One Russian leads to another, Roger plays a bassoon solo from Tchaikovsky's *Capriccio Italien*, and I am captivated.

The bassoon solo in the *Capriccio* covers only twelve measures, not long enough for a final piece. But there is an oboe solo soon after it that has a nice melody, and blaring trumpets open the work. With the versatility of the bassoon, maybe I can knit the three parts together and make something of it.

This could be a good mini-medley. The forte clarion call of the trumpet phrase brings to mind a triumphant Roman legion marching through a stone archway after conquering yet another city-state. That leads seductively to the bassoon part, played *ritenuto*, suddenly slow, and is more than a little mysterious and dramatic, conjuring up the image of a lone couple entwined in a sultry tango embrace in a shadowy cellar club somewhere in Argentina. Then comes the oboe solo, light and airy, more like being in Umbria a long time ago for a country dance at harvest time in the piazza of a small town with its dry, cracked central fountain and ancient, worn cobblestones. To finish the excerpt, there is a return to a solitary trumpet-like blast on a high A.

I have never composed anything except a corny, yet heartfelt country-western love song to my wife shortly after we were married. But undeterred, I find some five-line music paper and set out to write the mini-medley for my *Capriccio Perché No*.

When I am done writing down the notes, I realize that I haven't put in the key signature, the tempo, or the bars that separate one measure from another. If you have ever seen those gigantic Gregorian chant tomes in Gothic cathedrals, with square neumes for notes, you will know what my score looked like.

I decide it seems like a 6/8 rhythm, so I put in bars here and there, copy the D major signature that Tchaikovsky chose, and send it off to Roger to see what he thinks.

He is very kind, and without an audible guffaw, he does nevertheless mention that 6/8 time means there have to be six beats to the bar, and some of mine only have five. He also is puzzled by the almost imperceptible difference in my composition between quarter notes and half notes. Nevertheless, he is able to divine my meaning and sends back a playable version.

The mini-medley is thirty-seven measures long, eighteen of which have rapid register changes from one octave to a higher one and back again. This proves my undoing. As time goes by, I can play everything fine except the octave shifts. I even get to the point where I am working on interpretation, following the dynamics, the swelling and subsiding of the music, and coloring the tone. Except for the octave shifts.

I take the lessons learned from teachers on the other instruments on how to practice and apply them to my bassoon sessions. I slow down to the point of taking it one note at a time, then add a note, then another until I build them into a phrase. I practice starting at different parts of the score. I practice the difficult transitions, especially the octave shifts on eighth notes, over and over and over again. I practice with a metronome and without one. I let a day go by without any practice.

The results are not encouraging. The clarinet and oboe have nice, reliable octave keys for changing from a low register to a higher one. Tap the key, and presto change-o, you play an octave higher.

Not so on the demon bassoon. There is, instead, the notorious half-hole. Only it is not half of a hole; it is a whole hole. But, to change octaves, you have to cover it only half-way. Or sometimes only a quarter of the way. Or an eighth of the way.

Now, if the half-hole were the size of a manhole cover, it would not be so hard to figure out the halves, quarters, or eighths. Dividing up a nice pumpkin pie into fractions, or even a penny, would be manageable.

But the diameter of my nemesis, the half-hole, is a measly 4mm, about the size of a single petit pois. The width of my left index finger on the other hand, the digit tasked with covering, or partially covering the half-hole, is a bulbous 15mm, almost four times as big. The mechanics of it do not incline in my favor. It is not quite as daunting as the physics-defying bumblebee, but a challenge akin to trying to slice that pumpkin pie into precisely four even pieces with the blade of a bulldozer.

It now seems that the more I practice, the worse I get. This is similar to the end game on the violin, and that ultimately turned out fine, so there is still hope. Or maybe I got cocky after the relative successes of the clarinet and oboe. Maybe Roger and I should have spent more time on fundamentals before diving headfirst into the *Capriccio* and, as he put it, "teaching me to the test."

My last lesson looms. I am less confident of playing the selection well than I was on any of the previous instruments, and I was never 100% confident on those. I warm up with scales and an easy étude and square myself up in my chair to play the capriccio medley. A false start. That's all right. Relax and start again. The first part sounds good, but when the octave shift eighth notes come, I flub one after another. I begin three more times without once playing the *Capriccio* straight through without an octave shift hiccup. Not good. Not reasonably listenable.

*Is this what it feels like to fail?* A bit of a panic sensation, with no hope of changing the outcome. Failure is hard to swallow. What do I do with this failure? Failure, if taken the wrong way, can send you into a downward spiral that is hard to climb out of. Taken the right way, it means nothing more than that you failed in attempting to do something that you set out to do, but it does not mean that *you* are a failure. There is a big difference.

For example, I failed to play the *Capriccio Italien* on the bassoon in a reasonably listenable fashion in twelve lessons. That is a fact. I failed to do it—an indisputable fact. And that makes me frustrated, sad, and angry. Yet as I mull over my failure maybe, just maybe, it is not a total failure. Perhaps I just failed at the *Capriccio*. To find out, I get the sheet music arranged for the bassoon of the Promenade from Modest Mussorgsky's *Pictures at an Exhibition*. It also has octave shifts but not as many or as difficult.

*Voilà!* In two practice sessions, I can play the *Promenade* from start to finish better than I ever played the *Capriccio*.

The conclusion I reach is that the piecemeal medley that my teacher and I stitched together from the Tchaikovsky was just very ambitious, more advanced, and too difficult for me to learn in the allotted time. It is in A major with three sharps, while the Mussorgsky is in F major with only one flat. It is much easier. So, the work that I put in trying to get the *Capriccio* right served me well in being able to play another piece of absolutely lovely music in a reasonably listenable fashion. By moving the goalpost a little closer, I was able to score.

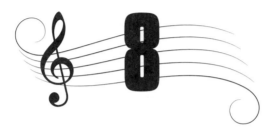

# The Flute

"I've never had that happen before," Cathy Peterson blurts out at my third flute lesson. She is an excellent teacher with twenty-nine years of experience, but apparently I am her first student to be able to not play a middle C.

Being *able to not play* the middle C is different from *not being able to play* it. It is all about where you put the *not*. Being able to not play it is a bit of a specialty. It means I am very good at not playing the middle C; no matter what I try or how hard I try, I cannot play it.

On the other hand, not being able to play it sort of implies a 'yet.' Not being able to play the middle C, yet. It is very possible that over-thinking the point of distinction between where the *not* goes is contributing to the problem.

There is also a mathematical aspect of my early difficulties with the flute that I am literally not quite grasping. The geometry of a tripod is generally thought to be a stable figure, its three points preventing whatever it is holding from teetering over in one direction or another. But when the tripod consists not of three sturdy legs of steel or wood but rather your lower lip, left thumb, and right pinky, the dependable tripod feels more like a slippery jellyfish.

Cathy is a bit concerned and gently suggests instead of waiting the customary week before our next session, that we have a remedial lesson the very next day. She suggests it the same way a good doctor might "suggest" a bronchial inhaler when a patient comes wheezing into the office snorting like a wild boar in heat.

I am told *not* to do anything, including touching the flute, until our remedial lesson, lest I exacerbate the problem and make it even harder to correct. This not is very clear and requires no thought, only obedience.

The whole idea of a remedial lesson sends me back to elementary school, where there was a remedial reading teacher named Hazel. Hazel was short and thin, stooped, with a beak of a nose and brittle grey hair like straw that stuck out sideways from her head and made her look very much like every fourth-grader's stereotyped idea of a witch. This, of course, earned her the nickname Witch Hazel, which would send me and my classmates into paroxysms of laughter whenever we saw Witch Hazel walking down the hall toward us.

The remedial lesson seems to head me in the right

direction, even if it doesn't solve the problem right away. I still can't play the C, but Cathy gives me a work-around so we can move onward. We won't play any exercises with a C. It seems to me a little like painting a seascape without a tube of blue paint, but I may have learned something about expectations from the overly ambitious bassoon experience, so I am letting her dictate the process.

I have my own Theory of Expectations, which has nothing to do with the financial one that tries to predict what short-term interest rates will be, based on long-term interest rates. Mine is more pedestrian but far more useful. It says that when reality matches your expectations, you feel that life is good. When it doesn't match them, you feel out of sorts, disappointed, and disgruntled. It is safe to start with low expectations and then be pleasantly surprised if things turn out better than you thought they would. A job interview that you believe is a long shot but for which you get an offer or a tough test in college that looks at best like a C that you actually ace are examples of reality exceeding expectations.

It is less safe to turn this approach upside down and have high expectations only to have them dashed by the cold facts of reality. I did just that with the bassoon and am vowing not to repeat it with the flute.

The instruments are so radically different that I find myself grinning at the contrast. Imagine being at the zoo and gawking at the hippos. You close your eyes, and when you open them again, you are in front of a canary. Everything is so much more delicate, refined, and elegant. I like hippos, too, and I am not saying that one is better than the other;

quite the contrary. The prodigious diversity in nature, as well as in the orchestra, is what, in the best of circumstances, produces the great harmony that both are capable of.

Even the posture is different for playing the flute. You are more or less reading the music looking over your left shoulder rather than straight on. Because of this, the music is on your left, and your instrument is on your right. Straight ahead is the empty corner of the room.

Because of this, having good peripheral vision is an asset in learning the flute. With the clarinet, oboe, and bassoon, you can see, or at least sense, where your hands and fingers are because they are in front of you when you play. Not so with the flute. Your fingers are off to the side, mainly out of view.

Initially, it is quite awkward, a little like your first day would be if you were a mailman with a rural delivery route, sitting on the passenger side of the car so you can reach the mailboxes with your right hand, but steering the car with your left way over on the driver's side.

The chromatic progression of notes, up or down the scale, is also markedly different from the other woodwinds. Although there are exceptions, to go down the scale on the clarinet, oboe, and bassoon, you progressively press down one finger after another on holes, levers, or keys, and to go up the scale, you lift them up.

The flute is not quite so intuitive, and I find in my practicing that there are longer pauses between note changes than the music says there should be. I struggle to figure out where to put my fingers.

Cathy gives me a flash card drill, and I enlist my wife,

Doyen, to drill me. She holds up a card with a note on it, say C sharp. Then in random order, she holds up another note, maybe A flat. My job is to mentally process what I see on the card and play that note on the flute. It is very slow at the beginning, as the message from the card has to pass through what seems like a bowl of molasses in my brain before I interpret it and can play the note. But practice makes almost perfect, and the pace picks up. Soon the cards really begin to fly by as Doyen unveils and discards one after another like a magician at a kid's birthday party.

Being able to quickly recognize the notes has an immediate impact on my playing, and a certain fluidity begins to emerge.

Cathy is aware of what happened with the bassoon and is purposefully leading me very slowly on the flute. It is having a calming effect. We have not selected an end piece, so there is nothing to measure progress against. I can't assess whether or not I am approaching "reasonably listenable" because I don't know what the piece is. Instead, we work on tone in the low and middle registers and how changing the shape of the embouchure changes octaves. Cathy encourages me to put a mirror on the music stand so I can see my embouchure. The mirror itself is a stark reality check, and it is wise to concentrate on my mouth and blot out the rest of what stares back at me unmercifully. It is effective, though, in much the same way that a ballerina can self-correct a position or pose by watching herself in the mirrored walls in her dance studio.

Once Cathy shows me what a good embouchure looks like, I try to imitate it in the mirror. Often, I think my embouchure is right only to produce a thin, unpleasant tone. Check in the mirror, and sure enough, I am either not centered on the mouthpiece hole, or my lips are not forming the right shape.

Little adjustments make a big difference in the tone, as does the direction of the air. Making a buck-toothed Bugs Bunny face helps prepare for the high notes, and a bit of a thin Mona Lisa smile works better for the low ones. Breathing starts way down in your stomach as you inhale with an open mouth to sound like Darth Vader.

Making all these faces in the mirror is a little freakish. I startle at the recollection of my father when I witnessed him having a stroke. His face went into unrecognizable contortions, a rubber-faced parody of a silly circus clown changing in an instant to the grotesque leer of Goya's charcoal drawings of men in hell. It was by turns comical and frightening to see my minimally expressive father doing this unconsciously. My brother and I rushed him to the hospital, and by the time we got there, he was feeling somewhat better but with no memory of what had happened to him. Fortunately, he recovered from that stroke and lived many happy years afterward.

These thoughts nevertheless cycled through my mind as I worked on loosening my upper lip, un-sticking it from my teeth with the bunny face, and relaxing my neck muscles for smoother airflow. I really didn't think that taking music lessons would involve things like this.

Yet Cathy knows what she is doing, and focusing on technique first and foremost for half of our twelve lessons is continuing to pay dividends. I've learned from coaching baseball that you play the way you practice. A casual, not-so-great focus or effort during practice ingrains that standard into your muscle memory, and you end up playing the same way in a game. The results are not good. For high-level performance, you cannot turn the juice on and off like a faucet. You have to practice with purpose.

Conscious of this, and even though many of the exercises and études are far from heavenly music, I approach them as if they were and try to play each note, each phrase with as lovely and pure a tone as I can. It is a challenge because they include difficult fingering, slurs and tonguing, octave shifts, high scales, and low scales. I consciously remind myself that focusing on the process rather than on the goal is sometimes the best approach. I sense that I am slowly yet inexorably moving away from the breathiness of the early lessons and toward how a modern flute should sound.

That breathy sound was bred out of the flute as it developed from the primitive hollowed-out or desiccated bone flutes played by people from the Paleolithic period some 40,000 years ago. Only drums pre-date the flute as a purpose-built musical instrument. The earliest flute, eight and a half inches long with five holes, came from the bone of a Griffin vulture and was found by archaeologists in Germany. One entry I saw as I researched the origins of the flute stated in all seriousness that those five Paleolithic holes were drilled by hand.

Notwithstanding the brilliance of that deduction, the presence of flutes in the daily life of Neanderthals casts them in a substantially different light than the conventional and erroneous image of a stooped and hunched, hairy hominid carrying a club.

Those Neanderthals had culture. They may even have had a wind ensemble. The vulture flute players would take the high melody line, saber tooth tiger femurs would provide the midrange harmonies, and a couple of hefty guys with their prized Wooly Mammoth tusks would rumble out an earth-shaking ground bass.

The flute certainly has come a long way, although it took a long time to mature, longer than most other instruments. Renaissance flutes were what we call recorders now and still had a somewhat breathy sound.

In some cultures, the breathy quality has endured and become a genre of its own. The ubiquitous folk musicians from Otavalo, Ecuador, with their quenas and cane pan pipes, seem to pop up in the most unexpected places, enveloping themselves and listeners alike in a bubble of haunting melodies. I have heard them busking in San Jose, Costa Rica, Edinburgh, Scotland, and Boulder, Colorado.

Native American flute music, likewise, crops up in a variety of places, some far from its roots in the American Southwest. Bookstores, spas, and art galleries seem to be partial to the calming sound and the long, impressionist phrases of the native flute.

Where that calming effect is really needed, though, is in the dentist's office and during the interminable hold times on a help line while you wait to find out how to work the four TV remotes lying mutely on your lap.

Wondrously, you can find serendipity with flute music away from the concert hall. Years ago, on a sandbar campsite, while rafting down the wide Green River in Utah, it was close to sunset, and the waning, hot summer sun shone its roseate rays of light on the soft, red cliff walls. As the water lapped against the shore and the swallows darted through the still air, one of the boatmen, a slim, darkly tanned, Japanese-Hawaiian man who could have been anywhere from forty-five to sixty-five years old, climbed up barefoot to a rock outcrop. There he sat, cross-legged and bare-chested, and played his Native-American flute. Without the music, it would have been merely a pretty sunset. But the breathy, hollow, improvised flute was so much a part of the natural setting at that moment that it had a strong emotional impact, evoking a past beyond personal memory that left a strong musical imprint.

At our sixth lesson, the halfway mark on our journey to "reasonably listenable," Cathy is satisfied with my technical progress and unveils the end piece. It will be the Intermezzo from Georges Bizet's *Carmen Suite #1*. She also throws in a Händel *Minuet*. This woman is showing confidence in me and it is catching. I am also beginning to feel it.

I can now say that I am playing the flute. But I am not sure what that makes me. With the cello, I was an aspiring cellist, and with the oboe, a beginner oboist. But it is not as simple with the flute. Am I a *flutist* or a *flautist*?

It seems to depend more on geography than meaning. One flutist can be just as good as another flautist. In America, flutist prevails, while the English prefer flautist, even though in a bit of reverse snobbery, the word flutist appeared first in a 1603 edition of the Oxford English Dictionary. Flautist did not appear until around 1880, some 275 years later. It is a bit pretentious to use flautist in America, but it's perfectly OK, as long as you know you are being pretentious, which in the right company can be good for a tongue-in-cheek laugh. If, for instance, you happen to be stuck in a pseudo-sophisticated concert intermission conversation with someone who wants desperately to impress anyone within earshot, you might respond to him (it is always a him) and his imperious pronouncements by saying, "Yes, I quite see your point, but it pales in comparison to the inner voice of the superb flautist in the second movement scherzo." To which he will clearly see he is over matched and quickly ask if anyone would like a second drink.

Perhaps James Galway, the legendary Irish flutist, said it best when he quipped, *"I am not a flautist; I don't have a flaut, and I've never flauted."*

There is another flute conundrum that, while not being serious enough to keep me awake at night, is nevertheless puzzling. Why is a flute a woodwind?

The flute is considered a woodwind instrument even though it is not made of wood, in the same curious way that a football is considered a ball even though it is not round and certainly is not made from a foot. A football is thrown and caught like a ball and kicked as part of the game, so it makes sense that it gets its "ball" name from the way it is used.

Renaissance flutes were made of wood, so the name-makers can be excused for holding on to an archaic nomenclature even as the preferred flute material evolved to nickel, silver, and gold.

Another reason the flute is a woodwind is because it

produces sound more like the way other woodwinds do than the way brass instruments do.

All woodwinds have keys and holes, and the sound comes either from a reed that vibrates as the player blows, or, in the case of the flute, by splitting the air blown across the lip plate. The sound emerges multi-directionally from holes all over the instrument as vibrating air escapes in different combinations of keys, pads, and holes. Brasses, by contrast, are unidirectional. All the sound emerges from the bell at the end of various configurations of tubing, and the vibrations come not from the instrument but from the musicians' lips.

As we move closer to the end, I realize that, except for the inauspicious beginning, the flute has been the most uneventful instrument to learn. It is my Golden Retriever instrument. Goldens are so calm, responsive, cooperative, and undemanding. If you treat them right, you are very likely to have a wonderful time together. That is what I am finding with the flute.

The flute works *with* you, it wants you to succeed, and it rewards you. If you relax, the sound will be good. I realize that I am playing more musically, producing a better tone than I have on the other instruments I have waded through, except for the clarinet, which is the one instrument I had played before.

I am also understanding phrasing better and playing smoother, which comes, in part, from a scanning approach to reading the music. If you look only at the note you are about to play, the sound is choppy and disconnected. If you train yourself to look a few notes or a measure ahead, you can play more smoothly and still be accurate.

It is the same idea as looking ahead a few steps on a rocky trail in the mountains instead of looking down at your feet. By doing so, in both cases, you gain a certain momentum that keeps you moving forward and well-balanced. Crossing a stream on a log or single plank bridge is the same thing. If you look ahead, your feet will know where to go, but if you look down at your feet, you are likely to teeter or even fall.

This affinity for the flute comes as a surprise because I had absolutely no attraction to the flute ahead of time. I never thought of playing it, never sought out flute recordings for my music collection, and yet I find it a soothing, comforting instrument. I feel relaxed playing it, maybe in part because of the way I have to breathe to get the right tone. To me, it is like a sigh; there is no back-pressure as there is in the reed instruments.

This feeling is contrary to how most people think of flute players and how many flute players think of themselves. They are regarded as high-energy, sometimes high-strung, competitive people, especially in contrast to the stereotypically easy-going and agreeable nature of bassoonists, or the equally stereotyped fastidious and precise oboe players.

To add to the cartoon-like characters that make up the orchestra, there are the brash and bombastic brass guys, the barely noticeable, wallflower violists, the I-get-the-best-parts violins, the mellow cello folk, the solid, you-can-count-on-me bassists, and the real cut-ups in the orchestra, the percussionists.

Cathy has recorded a piano accompaniment to the Bizet

and Händel pieces, and the approach of my last lesson has the feeling of a recital. I am a tad nervous but have been letting the beauty of the music carry me past my technical concerns. I listen to a few recordings of the Bizet Intermezzo solo and know how it is supposed to sound.

I carry that thought throughout the day and have the most peaceful dream that night. I am playing the flute and riding on a cloud, swaddled in cloth like a cherub in a Raphael painting. I awake soothed and relaxed, and confident.

All goes well at the lesson, which is held outdoors in Cathy's backyard. The music, unconstrained by walls, seems to be lifted from the flute and wafted away into the air. My overactive imagination sees a colorful display of Disney-inspired songbirds pausing on branches, heads cocked, listening to me play. When I finish playing, Cathy stands, and with a warm smile and her head cocked to one side apprecia-tively, gives me a gentle round of applause.

I like the flute well enough to become a little melancholy at the thought of leaving it behind. There is irony in the limited lesson rubric I set up as part of learning the instru-ments and writing the book.

I decided on it somewhat arbitrarily, calculating how many instruments multiplied by how many weekly lessons equals how many years and months to complete the cycle. I scribbled numbers on a yellow pad and found the twelve-lesson equa-tion to be the most reasonable. Eleven instruments x 12 weeks = 132 weeks ÷ 52 weeks in a year = two and a half years.

But I am finding that twelve lessons puts me just on the cusp of being really about ready to play the instrument fairly well. Just when I am beginning to feel comfortable on one, for me to play *it* rather than it playing *me*, I have to move on to the next one.

The last lesson is behind me, but I still have the flute in the house. I am curious to see if I am only a two-trick pony and can just play the Bizet Intermezzo solo and the Händel *Minuet* or if I really learned to play the flute.

I am a lifelong Gilbert and Sullivan fan, and I rummage through some old boxes to find a music anthology of all the G&S operettas. I haven't looked at it for years, but it is familiar and thick. I take the flute out of the case that I thought I had closed for good and randomly start sight-reading the vocal line from the scores. It is pure joy. I don't play the tunes perfectly; after all, I am a dilettante, but I play passably well, especially for sight-reading.

Page after page, song after song, my fingers find the notes almost automatically, and I can transition from low to mid to high registers and back as the music demands, relaxed and with confidence.

Time stands still, and when my embouchure finally gives out, I look up and see that it is past midnight. So, time did not stand still at all: I had played for almost three hours. It was as close to being in a musical zone as I have been with any of the instruments.

When I do finally put the flute away and close the lid for the last time, it is with the same satisfaction as tucking a child into bed for the night, pulling up the covers, and placing a gentle kiss on their brow to send them off to dreamland.

# Second Interlude

Now that I have had a taste of playing seven instruments, I hunger for something more. I have been daydreaming about how gratifying it would be to play one of them in an orchestra. Of course, I don't know which one I would play, or more truthfully, which one I could play, even up to the standards of an average community orchestra.

Then one day, the daydream takes on the blush of a possibility.

Alexander McCall Smith is a highly successful author, most famous for his series, *The No.1 Ladies Detective Agency*. This Scotsman from Edinburgh, a bioethicist and professor of medical law, has literally written over four score books, mostly fiction, which have sold more than forty million copies worldwide. His stories always have happy endings, and he has a treasure chest of jeweled ideas from which he seems to extract pearls of wit and wisdom at will.

He also loves classical music and is an amateur bassoonist. One day, at a school concert in which one of his children performed, he noticed how much fun the kids were having. Why can't we adults do the same, he thought. Why can't we experience the same joy of making music together, even if we are not professional musicians? Why not, indeed?

Finding nothing suitable for him to join, he and his wife decided to organize their own orchestra.

There was no problem in assembling enough like-minded people around Edinburgh for a decent-sized ensemble, complete with strings, woodwinds, brass, and percussion, but there was a problem. When they got together to rehearse, they realized that they were really not very good. In fact, they were pretty bad. Wrong notes were sounded, the rhythms were inconsistent, the reeds squeaked, and the pitch of the strings was all over the place. Rather than struggle to improve, and with the encouragement of their leader, Alexander McCall Smith, they accepted their fate and christened themselves as the RTO, the Really Terrible Orchestra.

This is music to my ears. I think I can play with this orchestra. Reasonably Listenable and Really Terrible are quite compatible.

I wonder how bad they really can be and, in poking around, come upon a somewhat apocryphal story that I suspect puts whatever doubts I may have had to rest.

It seems that at a break at one rehearsal, a double bass player came up to the conductor and told him she was puzzled. Page 19 of her score says the music is in 3/4 time but he is conducting it in 4/4 time.

The conductor asks to see her score and, after a moment, tells her she is absolutely right, her score is in 3/4 time, but it is not the piece they are playing.

I *know* I can play with this orchestra.

I manage to locate the music director of the RTO in Scotland, Richard Neville-Towle. He is a real musician and conductor, and I send him an email outlining the idea of this book, and, to my surprise, he replies. He says that the RTO and I are clearly kindred spirits and invites me to come and watch a rehearsal. I am thrilled but demur since I am 4,000 miles away across one ocean, two mountain ranges, and half a continent.

But I can still imagine what it might be like to play with the RTO.

Franz Joseph Haydn wrote his *Symphony No. 45*, the *Farewell* symphony, as a not-so-subtle message to his patron, Prince Esterházy, that he was keeping the orchestra at the palace and away from their families far longer than he had agreed upon.

*No. 45* sounded to the prince like a normal Haydn symphony until the last section of the final movement, an adagio. At that point, as the music rolled along toward its conclusion, something quite different happened. At the performance for the Prince, and under Haydn's direction, one by one, the players blew out the candles by their music stands and left the hall. First, a French horn departed, then a few violins, followed soon after by the double basses and more winds. The musicians just stood up, and with wisps of smoke from their extinguished candles trailing behind them, and without so much as a "by your leave," they left the room. By the final measure, all that remained were two lonely violins. The prince got the message and dismissed the orchestra the next day to return to their families.

What I picture is that the RTO is playing the Haydn *Farewell*, and I am playing with them in the French horn section. As the horns get up to leave, I look around, put down my horn, move over to the oboes, change instruments, and start playing the oboe. When they depart, I do the same thing, leave the oboes and sidle over to the next section and play the cello. I keep moving from one instrument to another as I continue to be abandoned by one section after another. At the end, there is just me and that one other lonely violin.

Now, I could not do that with just any orchestra, but given the *bona fides* of mediocrity earned by the RTO, it would add more interest to the concert and probably not diminish their already tarnished reputation.

*What do they, or I, have to lose?*

With more than a touch of bravado, I send off an email with that suggestion to the Chairman of the RTO, Mr. Ninian Hewitt.

The bad news is that I have not heard a word from Messrs. Hewitt or Neville-Towle. The good news is that they have not yet taken back their invitation to a rehearsal.

# The Trombone

For the first time, I am taking lessons from a friend, Jon Stubbs, so there is more than a purely professional student-teacher relationship at stake. I have seen him teach and I know he is good. But can a couple of men who have been comfortable as equals for many years adapt to the unequal roles of teacher and student? Will I accept his trombone demands even though with anything else we do he has little chance of ordering me about and even less of me blindly obeying? Or will he go too easy on me so he doesn't risk losing our friendship?

We discuss this before the first lesson, and I ask him to promise he will treat me as he would any other student and not compromise his musical standards for the sake of our friendship. In return, I promise I will not dispute his decisions and keep my mouth shut, except for when I am playing.

He agrees and puts our understanding to the test right away by saying I should get rid of my rental trombone and get a different one. The one I have is no good. I start to say something, then stop. What he just did was prove to me that he will maintain a high standard and not just think, "Oh, that's good enough for Jim; he's just going to take twelve lessons, so who cares." I say not a word.

The trombone is unlike the other brasses, namely the trumpet, French horn, and tuba. The trombone has no keys, just a long, twenty-two-inch slide. Coincidentally, that is the same distance from my shoulder to my fingertips.

There is nothing as certain as pressing a key to play the right note. Instead, the player relies on developing a kinesthetic sense of where their arm has to be relative to the extension of the slide to produce the desired note.

There are some visual cues, but you can't always rely on them when you are reading music at the same time. By practicing intervals with first position as your base, the position with the slide all the way in, close to your mouth, you try to develop muscle memory in your right arm.

With your elbow as the hinge, you push the slide just a bit further out for second position. Third is fingers aligned just before the bell. Fourth is just beyond the bell. Fifth is with a slight curve at the elbow and hand. Sixth is arm out straight with your hand cocked at a right angle. Seventh is stretching your right arm and hand all the way out as far as they will go.

The idea is to make the positions familiar enough so you do not need to think about them, much in the way that you can navigate your way through your house or apartment in the dark because you know instinctively where everything is.

I am practicing those intervals at a lesson, playing an exercise that calls for going from first position, close to my mouth, back and forth to each of the other positions three times apiece for a total of twenty-one times. The movement has to be quick and precise to produce clean, crisp note changes. It is what you see when you watch a good trombonist; in and out, in and out.

First through fourth positions are a piece of cake, within easy reach, and I am nailing the pitch, too. Fifth is an in-between position, and I get it right two out of the three times. Sixth comes out fine, as it is a very mechanical move with a straight arm and the wrist at a ninety-degree angle.

Seventh position is a stretch. It is difficult, but I am getting it until the twenty-first and last move of the whole exercise. Then, with a sudden, confident thrust to seventh position, I lose control of the slide altogether and sling it across the room with the speed of William Tell shooting his arrow at the apple on top of his son's head.

The slide whooshes through the air, barely missing Jon, and skids across the floor, coming to a quivering stop just short of the wall. I am left standing with half a trombone in my left hand and nothing at all in my right. There is a moment of stunned silence before Jon and I burst into somewhat goofy laughter. Despite this unfortunate incident, the trombone survives its trauma, and we continue.

The proverbial wise man once said that experience is a good teacher, and I am learning that it is true. Through experience, I now have a better understanding of how to practice: slow down, especially with the hard passages, and separate the music into small chunks. Trying too hard when things do not go well makes you tense, and then nothing goes right. Relax. Play measures backward sometimes. Don't start at the same spot all the time. Practice slurs, tonguing, and legato, and make producing a good tone a priority with everything.

Even though practicing better motivates me to practice more and to focus harder, there are still struggles. The preliminaries before working on the end piece can get tedious.

If the whole practice continuum were plotted on a graph, the process would look like a reverse bell curve. Instead of lows at both ends and a nice, long, upward thrust to a peak in the middle, I start high, elated by the wonderment of something new, and typically make fast progress. To me, that is always an exciting time, whether it is a new instrument, traveling someplace new, or eating at a new restaurant.

Then comes the plunge in the curve, a trough that is sometimes prolonged and deep. The challenge and frustration of always trying to play better can be discouraging. It is slow progress, plowing through seemingly endless pages of exercises, scales, and études. They are designed to build competency and are, by their very nature, repetitive. But I have to do it; there are no shortcuts, at least none that work. It is the hardest part.

Sometimes there is a "Eureka!" moment when everything

clicks, but more often it is a gradual, step-by-step climb out of the depths of the reverse bell curve up to the top again. With eventual improvement, the excitement does return, and I feel rejuvenated and rewarded by the effort.

Experience has also taught me that when I learn something new, I have to apply myself to the task not just with determination but with regularity. With just twelve lessons for each instrument, I cannot afford downtime and so even when I travel, I take whatever I am playing with me.

It was an easy one-hander with the flute, clarinet, or oboe cases, leaving the other hand free for a suitcase, computer bag, or deli sandwich. Travel was less carefree, yet still manageable with the bassoon case, but it took more planning with the cello. Do you wear it like a backpack and risk bumping it in a doorway, or carry it like a big guitar? Still, with a little care and attention, you can avoid normal hazards.

The double bass was a different story. It was a flat-out challenge to maneuver it along narrow corridors and around corners without cracking it against walls or other obstructions. When the double bass was developed in the 16th century, the grand palaces of Europe must have had much wider passageways than our abodes today.

One positive aspect of lugging around a heavy, fifty-pound double bass in its case, is its weight-bearing and aerobic exercise benefit. The ultimate test was hauling my bass up and down the forty-six steep stairs to get from our rental cottage on the shore of Grand Lake in Colorado to the road above, at an elevation of 8,400 feet.

After that, the trombone, in its case, was not a problem at

Grand Lake, although blowing it at 8,400' was. The thinner air had me gulping like a fish out of water. I found that I had to take more breaths and change the phrasing of what I was playing so I did not run out of air.

The Grand Lake trip was by car, so packing the trombone was easy. Being invited by my *"Slapstick"* brother Jerry to visit him at his home on Kiawah Island in South Carolina presents a different decision tree to climb. I cannot, in good conscience, subject him and his wife to my daily trombone practice sessions, but I do not want to lose a full week of playing while I am away.

"Buzz it," says Jon at our next lesson. Translated, that means just take the mouthpiece, and use my embouchure to play it, something like a kazoo.

"You can do scales, arpeggios, even tunes."

I take his advice and put the mouthpiece in my pocket for the flight to South Carolina.

In Kiawah, Jerry's library is on the second floor of the house, which sits elevated at the edge of a marsh. They do not use the "S" word in this part of the Carolina Low Country, as it is known to the thousands of Pat Conroy readers. The forbidden "S" word is swamp, and folks here are quick to point out that a swamp is a mass of decaying earth, while a marsh is healthy and teeming with life and vegetation.

The library is far enough away from the other rooms in the house for me to practice buzzing the mouthpiece without disturbing anyone.

In the library, I am surrounded by collections of Anthony Trollope, whose work my brother loves but is to me as tedious as picking dog hair off a fleece jacket or untangling last year's Christmas tree lights. The man can spend three pages describing dust motes caught in a shaft of light.

There are also Laurence Durrell first editions and 17th-century duodecimos from the press of the Dutch printer Elsevier, plus other biblio-treasures. I expect to find the slapstick from his *Sleigh Ride* performance enshrined in a glass display case commemorating his reaching the apex of his musical career, but it is nowhere to be seen.

It should be musty in there amidst those old books, but the room is filled with low country sunshine that inspires me to try buzzing Southern classics such as *Camptown Races* and *Old Folks at Home*. It is my first attempt at buzzing tunes, and the sound comes out like a flustered Donald Duck. It makes me laugh so hard that I have to pull a Trollope novel off the shelf and read a few paragraphs in order to settle down and regain my composure.

Buzzing makes me concentrate on the embouchure because without the slide and the rest of the trombone, it is the only way I can change notes. Big intervals come easier than small ones, arpeggios clearer than scales. As the days go by, my control improves, and I play by ear whatever pops into my head. I can sense the value of this kind of practice and am eager to see how well it will translate back to the full trombone when I get home. Practicing still sounds like Donald Duck, but this time an appealing Donald, so while taking a break, I glance out the window to see if any mallards have landed on the marsh.

The week passes quickly with bike riding and body

surfing at the beach, some tennis, laughter, good conversation, and plenty of great seafood filling the time between buzzing sessions.

Back home at my next lesson, Jon says he thinks it is time to choose the end piece. He makes a couple of suggestions, but none ring true to me, and I offer to do some research before we decide.

I spend hours researching and listening to trombone solos and orchestral excerpts. What do I like and which ones can I play? Looking at scores and sheet music is part of the process, and while I am not by nature a scholar, I enjoy this and am even more invested in the process. This makes me feel as much like a real musician as I may ever feel.

As soon as I hear the trombone excerpt from the overture to Richard Wagner's *Tannhäuser*, I know that this is it. It soars majestically, marked forte and double forte throughout, and within a range that I can play. The end pieces for previous instruments have been more lyrical: Bizet's Carmen *Intermezzo* for the flute, the adagio from Mozart's *Clarinet Concerto in A minor*, the *Swan Lake* oboe solo, and the Bach *Air on the G string* for the violin. By contrast, this one is bold and dramatic. It is less subtle and, therefore, should be somewhat easier to play well. It is the difference between tatting delicate Belgian lace and banging a Chinese gong with a four-foot mallet.

But there is an ethical dilemma I have to resolve first.

Wagner was an avowed and vociferous anti-Semite. He wrote a scathing diatribe as a young man and never recanted it as he matured. In fact, sticking to his views, he added more vitriol to it in his later years. To him, all Jews and Jewish composers, Mendelssohn in particular, could never be considered true artists. He even advocated that all Jews should be driven from Germany.

Wagner's detractors also cite characters in *Parsifal, Die Meistersinger*, and *The Ring Cycle* as examples of his ideology infiltrating his music. He was deliberate in creating anti-Semitic archetypes, well known to everyone at the time and meant to offend. While not officially banned, to this day you seldom hear any Wagner performed in Israel.

Adding to his dark reputation is the after-the-fact identification of Wagner with Nazism and Adolf Hitler, who praised Wagner as much, if not more, for his anti-Semitic views as for his music. The fact that Hitler was born six years after Wagner died doesn't seem to matter.

Wagner had an enormous ego, and he could not accept any of his many difficulties as being of his own making. He regularly and publicly blamed Jews and the Jewish community for his personal and financial woes.

Without belaboring the issue further, there is ample evidence that Wagner the man was a deplorable anti-Semite. It is indisputable. But what of his music? Is there such a thing as anti-Semitic music? Professor Alexander Knapp of the University of London, a Wagner scholar, says, "For me, music, per se, cannot be anti-Semitic. How can a chord or sequence of chords be anti-Semitic?"

If every time I heard music by Wagner I thought instantly and almost exclusively about his anti-Semitism, then the man and the music would be inextricably intertwined, and I would not play the *Tannhäuser* excerpt. But I don't think of it that way, and I don't believe that playing it condones his views or gives him a pass on being responsible for fanning the flames of the anti-Semitism of his times.

Were he alive today, or I then, it would be a different story. Every penny he earned from his music was then, and could be now, put to use to further his anti-Semitic activities directed at discrediting and destroying the reputations and lives of Jews, and I would have none of that.

Perhaps it is different in Israel and the Germany of today. I acknowledge that possibility and respect anyone who feels that way. In fact, I feel that way about the Civil War tune *Dixie*, which became the unofficial national anthem for the pro-slavery South. I cannot hear it without a knot tightening in my stomach.

My dilemma resolved, I propose the *Tannhäuser* excerpt to Jon and he endorses it, not Wagner, enthusiastically.

The preparation begins and the hard, technical study that preceded it is paying off. We work on tone first, to sustain the pitch on the notes at a tempo of 50 on a metronome. That is longer than a second for each quarter note and is both hard to do well and easy to hear if I go off-key. The slow tempo makes the music transparent, with no opportunity to cover up mistakes with speed. Even though the score is marked forte and double forte, there are crescendos and decrescendos within those markings. Like two colleagues, we discuss how it will give color and drama to the music if I can do it.

It comes together a little at a time until I gradually piece together all the phrases that at first I practiced separately.

I can now play the music non-stop from beginning to end.

I believe that I am done and feel satisfied, but Jon thinks otherwise. His idea is to take his mp3 digital audio file of the Berlin Philharmonic, conducted by none other than Hebert von Karajan, and play the *Tannhäuser* overture through a Bluetooth wireless connection on my four-foot-tall living room speakers. They make a big sound that will be nice to hear, I muse, but he says, "No, not just hear, you play along with them."

I blink stupidly for a few seconds and then get it. I am to be placed in front of the speakers with my trombone as if I were part of the Berlin Phil trombone section while Jon, baton in hand, leads me and the rest of the Berlin Philharmonic Orchestra in the overture.

Perhaps I should put on my tuxedo to complete the faux performance, but Jon is already tuning up the mp3 and is ready to start.

There is a long introduction before the trombones come in, and we have the volume cranked up high enough to rattle some pottery on top of the speakers. When Jon gives me the downbeat for my entrance, I honestly cannot hear anything coming out of my trombone. *Am I playing? Am I playing with my section mates? Am I playing in tune?*

It is simply overwhelming, and I realize how different it is to play alone or with a small ensemble than it is with a full orchestra. We try it again a few more times but without much improvement. I cannot hear both myself and the rest of the orchestra and follow Jon's conducting all at the same time.

It is a letdown, and I feel disappointed that I did not rise to the occasion. Disappointed but not discouraged. Perhaps it is putting too fine a point on it, but had this not been the last lesson, I believe that with more practice playing with an orchestral accompaniment, I would have been able to play along reasonably well.

I do not want to leave Jon on a sour note, neither literally nor figuratively, so to prove to myself and to him that I really can play the Wagner excerpt, I record it solo on my phone. I play it back, listen, then play it back again and again. There is something curious happening. After the third time, I realize what it is. It does not sound like me playing the trombone. It sounds like someone else. Someone better, and to me, it is a bit more than reasonably listenable. I send an audio file off to Jon and get this response, "Yes, that is better." Not an overwhelming endorsement of my trombone talent, but at least there is hope that he will still join me for coffee sometime.

# The Trumpet

Skipping lightly down a sunlit garden path lined with tulips, lilies, and daffodils, on a spring day under a clear, blue sky, with butterflies flitting from flower to flower and a gentle breeze lifting the scent of sweet woodruff into the air is what it feels like to me to play the trumpet.

Yes, it is the same trumpet whose clarion call leads elephants and camels onto the stage in the triumphal march from Verdi's *Aida*. The same trumpet that glints under white gloves as uniformed military bands march down aircraft carrier decks and in July 4th parades to a John Philip Sousa tune. The same trumpet as in Aaron Copland's *Fanfare for the Common Man*, which has served as the anthem of the

Olympic games and stirred the passions of athletes and fans around the world for years. The same mass of brass that covers the midfield in football game halftime shows.

The blare of the trumpet fills the chest and sets the jaw. It instills strength and power in players and listeners alike. Iconic trumpet parts, such as in Rossini's *William Tell* and Tchaikovsky's *1812* overtures, are not those dainty spring flowers and butterfly images that caress me as I take up the trumpet.

It is very odd. I am halfway through my twelve lessons with nary a bump in the road. No awkward beginnings, no reverse bell curves, no floppy lips. My teacher is Ryan Gardner, President of the International Trumpet Guild and an Associate Professor at the University of Colorado School of Music. He has mentored hundreds of graduate-level and professional players, and yet he says to me, "I've never had someone go so far so fast." I am stunned.

Who knows why, but Ryan and I click in our teacher and student relationship. I feel a little like I am a very eager and willing puppy, and he is my trainer. When he shows me something and asks me to do it, I get it right away and can replicate it. He even rewards me with an *Atta boy!* as encouragement, although he stops short of offering me a treat.

Could it be that this is the instrument I am meant to play? Was I a trumpeter in a past life? I am not sure I have had a past life, but I am also not sure that I have not.

Maybe I was blowing a sheneb for Tutankhamun, although it looked like a straightened ear trumpet, and according to contemporary accounts, it sounded more like the braying of a donkey. Hardly fitting entertainment for a pharaoh.

Yet that was an improvement on the really old trumpets, whose purpose was not to make pretty music but to scare off predators and enemies with grating and supernatural sounds.

Regardless of my trumpeting ancestry, I am sailing along. Even the harder high notes are sounding pretty good, and high notes can be the nemesis for musicians of very different stripes.

It is important to have confidence that you can reach any note you need to play and not fall into the trap of thinking, "Oh, no, here comes that high one; I hope I can reach it."

When singers warm up before a performance, or before rehearsing a role, or even at a lesson, they vocalize to notes higher and lower than they will actually use in their performance. In theory, which in this case is the same as in practice, if a soprano, for example, can vocalize to an E above high C, she can sing the high C called for in the score without straining.

The same applies to the trumpet. Ryan gives me exercises that go beyond what I am likely to need to play in any music I choose for my final piece.

I can get to those high notes in two ways: using only my embouchure or by using the valves. The fingering of the trumpet is deceptively simple. There are only three valves and you only use three fingers of one hand to play them. Compare those three valves to the nineteen keys, pads, levers, and holes on the flute, twenty-one on the oboe, twenty-two on the clarinet, and a whopping twenty-four on the bassoon.

Yet the trumpet has to be able to produce the same number of notes as the other instruments with only those three valves. At first, it seems a little like trying to write a book with only half the letters in the alphabet.

The three valves have seven possible fingering combinations. They are open, with no valves pressed, then 1 (the first finger on the first valve), 2, 1&2, 2&3, 1&3, and 1,2&3. In each one of these positions, my embouchure has to play six different notes without changing the fingering. To make the changes, I control the amount of air I blow, how fast I blow it, and through how small an aperture in my lips I blow. Six notes times seven positions means that with just those three valves, the trumpeter can, or hopes to play, forty-two notes.

As I continue to make progress, my practice sessions are getting longer and longer. After one particularly long session, I look in the mirror and notice a slight bulge in the center of my upper lip. It could be the beginning of what is commonly called trumpeter's wart, although it is not a wart. It is hyperkeratosis, the thickening of the lip due to the friction of the lip's vibrations against the mouthpiece.

It is nothing serious. In fact, it is rather like a badge of honor, a fraternity pin that shows I belong to the brotherhood of authentic trumpet players. It is slight enough that I really have to look closely to see it, in much the same way that a pre-adolescent boy might stare into the mirror looking for enough facial fuzz to confirm that he is ready for his first shave.

In some instances, however, hyperkeratosis can turn into the dreaded rupture of the orbicularis oris muscle, a serious condition that can only be remedied by surgery. The incomparable Louis Armstrong suffered from this disorder and had it surgically treated in 1935, missing an entire year afterward to recover and rehab his lip.

While learning about hyperkeratosis and the orbicularis oris, I stumble across yet another of the dangers of playing the trumpet. Unless the trumpet is cleaned regularly, mold and fungus can accumulate in the tubing. Those bacteria are then inhaled and can cause hypersensitivity pneumonitis, a lung disease. Might it be safer for me to take up hang gliding or running with the bulls in Pamplona?

Cleaning the trumpet suddenly becomes a high priority, and I set forth to do it with dispatch.

It is not all that difficult or complicated. In fact, it is very simple. You pull apart the tubes into five pieces, unless you also clean the valves, then it's six more pieces. You more or less toss them into the kitchen sink with a little dishwashing detergent and warm water. It is much like what mechanics or car tinkerers do when they pull apart a transmission or, on older cars, the carburetor. They drench the filthy contents, screws and all, in an awful, gunky, de-greasing ooze.

Next, you take a long wire snake device with brushes on either end and ream out the tubes of the trumpet as if you were unclogging a stopped-up drain. Then, you set all the pieces out on a drying rack next to the breakfast dishes and last night's wine glasses and leave them to drip dry.

It is my good fortune to be able to re-assemble the trumpet with no leftover parts, although I do have a scare when I cannot find the mouthpiece. It is not on the drying rack with the other parts and not in the sink, which I drained after the washing.

I am certain that I cleaned it with soap and water, along with the other parts. Even so, I check the trumpet case, the music stand, and the hallway between the music room and kitchen, but all to no avail.

It has to be somewhere, and while I wait for that somewhere to occur to me, I make myself a peanut butter and honey sandwich on good rye bread, wash it down with a glass of cold milk and brush the crumbs off into the sink. I am about to flip the switch on the garbage disposal when it suddenly hits me. *Don't flip that switch!* an inner voice commands. I pull my hand back and reach down into the drain. There it is, the mouthpiece, all by itself, and saved by sheer luck from being mangled beyond recognition by the whirling blades of the disposal. I give it a gentle rinse, dry it by hand, and put it out to dry with the rest of the trumpet.

Since I am moving along rapidly and with some success, Ryan and I discuss what to choose as an end piece. He suggests several possibilities, and I go home and listen to them. His trumpet aesthetic and mine are different, just as Jon's trombone recommendations were not aligned with mine.

I take the time to listen to a lot of trumpet solos and orchestral excerpts. I like some trumpet voluntaries and concerto solos, but they are beyond my ability. Narrowing the field down, I find two *Airs* by Henry Purcell, the Presto from George Frideric Händel's *Water Music*, and the Promenade from *Pictures at an Exhibition* by Modest Mussorgsky. I want Ryan's opinion on which one I might be able to get the upper hand on, so I take the sheet music with me to my next lesson.

Ryan looks them over and says they are all good. I ask which one he thinks I should do, and with no hesitation and a dismissive wave of a hand, he says, "Oh, why don't you just do all four of them?"

I wonder if I can work up four end pieces instead of just one, but his encouragement spurs me on, and I accept the challenge.

He observes that three of the four are from the Baroque period and asks if I have a particular affection for that epoch. I had not made the connection, so I have to stop and think. The fact is, I am not fond of the overly theatrical lace and brocade fashions of the day, nor the grandiose, scrolling architecture, nor the ornate furniture design. There is so much ornamentation and artificiality in everything that it is over-whelming. It is 17th-century conspicuous consumption, all superficiality and decadence. Those are not my core values.

I am, nevertheless, drawn to Baroque trumpet music. The musical embellishments seem to be not as excessive as their period brethren, and despite some flashy trills typical of the style, the Baroque trumpet cuts through the complications and delivers clear, flowing, melodic lines.

Most Baroque music was written on demand for royalty, the aristocracy, or the church. It was not until Beethoven pioneered and popularized public concerts in the 1800s that what we today call serious music reached well beyond palaces and grand estates.

Lucky was the Baroque composer who had a full-time

church or royal appointment. Yet he had little autonomy and was expected to cater to the musical whims of the king or prince, often at a moment's notice. He had to be able to compose in almost any musical form that could be imagined since he might receive a princely order, as if from the menu of a Chinese restaurant: "I'll start with the #4 (Gavotte), then one #7 (Sonata), and for the main course a #12 (Divertimento)."

Feast days, royal ascensions, birthdays, and saint's days were typical occasions to commission a new piece of music. Both Händel and Purcell composed music for the festival of St. Cecelia, who is the patron saint of music and so received homage, with compositions performed on her day, November 22.

It is surely a coincidence, but what a wonderful tradition it would be to combine a celebration of St. Cecilia's Day with the annual release of the Beaujolais Nouveau, always on the third Thursday of November, which most conveniently, also can be on the 22nd.

To be accepted into the salons and grand ballrooms of their employers and perform in front of other elites, the composers had to dress the part. Even if they were otherwise treated more like the downstairs servants than the musical giants that they were, they were expected to turn out looking as if they belonged upstairs

They wore knee breeches, long white hose, stiff, brocaded waistcoats, and jackets to emulate their patrons. Most striking of all, to our eyes today, were the large, white, flowing, wavy or curly, powdered wigs, or perukes as they were called at the time. They top off virtually every portrait of the famous composers of the Baroque era: Purcell, Händel, Bach, Vivaldi, Telleman, Couperin, Rameau, Albinoni, the Scarlattis, Corelli, and Pachelbel.

The powdered wig became a popular fashion trend after King Louis XIV of France took up the style. It was actually started by his father, Louis XIII, whose vanity led him to adopt the wig to cover his baldness, which began when he was only seventeen. Before that, naturally longish hair was deemed sufficiently kingly.

Fashion was not, however, the only reason the powdered wig took Europe by storm. What drove men to sport the almost ubiquitous, white-powdered wig was hair lice and syphilis. There was a scourge of syphilis rampaging through Europe in the mid-1600s, and the wigs covered the sores and baldness that the disease caused. Scented powder, often in lavender or orange, further disguised the pungent odor of the condition lying underneath.

We never think of that when we look at the portraits of the great Baroque composers. All be-wigged, they appear healthy, intelligent, some even likable and confident. There is nothing in my research to indicate that they were anything other than as they appeared. They were men of their day and followed the fashion of the day—a plague on those who would have us believe otherwise.

That is not to say that they all were upstanding, flawless paragons of virtue. Händel was reputed to have had a hot temper. The beginning and end of Henry Purcell's life had the makings of a grim, Dickensian novel. He was born in Devil's Acre, a London slum, and died of pneumonia after being locked out of his home in a storm by his wife. Henry was not responsible for the circumstances of his birth, but one wonders what he was up to that night that occasioned the beginning of his end.

If only the stones could talk. There was no inevitability in his fate, but some things are inevitable, as I soon find out.

I guess it was bound to happen. Sooner or later, it was bound to happen. My sunlit garden trumpet path has turned into a murky, entangling patch of dead, impenetrable, twisted vines, poisonous mushrooms, and stinging wasps.

Ryan has been away on vacation, and I have gone two weeks without a lesson. Händel, Purcell, and Mussorgsky are turning over in their graves as I butcher their music.

I don't know what it is. I can play all the notes, and I can hear in my head how I want the music to sound, but it is not coming out right. It is frustrating, and like most people, when I get frustrated, I tense up, which only makes matters worse.

Professional musicians tell me that in preparing a piece to perform, it takes them about fifty percent of the time to get it ninety percent right and the other fifty percent to get that last ten percent right.

While my percentages are different, I know what they mean, and I am experiencing it in spades. It all came so easily at first, but now that I am trying to refine the four pieces well enough to be at least reasonably listenable, I am stymied.

In desperation, I try the Five Step Program that my wife and I devised for our son when he was about four, and also had trouble matching what he could imagine doing with what he was actually able to do, often involving Legos.

*One, try it again.*

*Two, try harder.*

*Three, try a different way.*

*Four, go away and come back to it later.*

*Five, ask for help.*

I am up to five and looking forward to my next lesson.

When Ryan calls to say he is back, I want to schedule a lesson as soon as possible. The students at the University of Colorado are still on break, so Ryan says we can use the new recital hall the next day for the lesson. It is a gorgeous space with excellent acoustics. We open the door, and Ryan walks right down the center aisle and up onto the stage. He looks behind him, but I am not there. I am still hanging back behind the last row of seats. It didn't occur to me that I would be playing on the stage of the recital hall. I don't know where I thought I would play, but it wasn't there, in front of all those seats, even if they were empty.

But overcoming my initial hesitation and walking down the aisle feels like I am at my own wedding, and since that was a really grand day and a great feeling, something starts to swell inside me, and by the time I reach the stage, I am ready for my debut.

Helped by my suddenly positive attitude, Ryan diagnoses my problem, and easily following his suggestions, the darkness of the previous two weeks turns to light, and by the end of the lesson, I am playing with confidence to him as he stands at the back of the hall.

The path forward still has a few rough patches, but a week of practice goes well, and I am ready for my last lesson back in his studio. As Ryan listens to me warm up, I hear him say more or less to himself, "Today's going to be good." He is right. Not only good, but the best I have ever played all four pieces. The two by Purcell, the Händel, and the Mussorgsky, all ring out with clarity, accuracy, and musicality. His joy at hearing the payoff of just twelve weeks on the trumpet makes me feel elated, and the lesson ends with back-thumping hugs.

It is still a week before I can start the French horn, so I keep playing the trumpet daily in order to keep my lip in shape.

On its last evening with me, I lift the trumpet off its stand and go outside. I pretend I am on the ramparts of a frontier fort in 1850 (in reality, it is our kids' play fort built in 1987). The endless high plains reach unbroken to a distant, rouged sunset, signaling the end of another hot, dusty day on the prairie. Behind me, a faded, thirty-one star American flag, with its leading edge frayed by the wind, is ready to come down for the night. With a ramrod straight back, I lift the trumpet ever so slowly to my lips, and to the vast and empty sky, I play *Taps*.

# The French Horn

Feeling confident, if not downright cocky, after the way the trumpet ended, I am eager to start on the French horn. Returning the trumpet, I pick up a rental French horn at my favorite shop, run by a wonderful Japanese American couple who have become my friends over the course of this project.

Maya Tsuchiya, the technical expert, tells me it is good that the French horn is the last one for me to play because it is the hardest. Had I started with it, I might never have continued. Masashi, her husband, has a different opinion. He ranks the oboe as the hardest. And so it goes, an unresolved debate that has been going on for centuries.

In both cases, size matters. The oboe has the smallest

aperture amongst the woodwinds, and the French horn's aperture is the smallest of all the brasses, about the size of a straw. There is little margin for error, which makes both instruments harder to play than the other winds. It is analogous to threading a needle to sew on a button versus sticking your whole arm into the sleeve of your coat.

The horn's difficulty lies partly in its compact yet unwieldy construction. It looks a lot like a Celtic knot, a labyrinthine path of narrow brass tubes interweaving and coiling devilishly around themselves. Were it not for the fact that it makes such an exquisite sound, it could be mistaken for some sort of steampunk contraption that could blow iridescent, beachball size soap bubbles or a tortuous machine with little ball bearings rattling noisily through the convoluted tubes.

If you were to unknot all the tubing of the French horn, it would stretch to about twelve feet, and if it is a double horn like the one I have, it would be closer to eighteen feet. As complex looking as it is, it is still comfortable to hold sitting down, with the rim of the bell resting on your thigh.

My double horn is like a twofer, two horns in one. One set of twisted, intestine-like tubing is tuned in F and is for lower notes. The other is in B-flat for higher notes. You shift from one set of tubes to the other by using a trigger key with your left thumb. It works very like, but not exactly like the octave keys on the clarinet and oboe.

I learn before my first lesson that my teacher, Michael Robert Thornton, the Principal French horn for the Colorado Symphony and the Los Angeles Chamber Orchestra, will play the gorgeous horn solo in the Tchaikovsky *Symphony No. 5*. I buy a ticket and get to the concert early, like a groupie at a rock concert. Settling into my seat with binoculars in hand, I scan the horn section for the principal and gulp hard when I spot Mr. Thornton. From my vantage point, he appears to be a bloodless, stern-looking man who has never seen the sun or learned to smile. He is all business as he sits and arranges the music on his stand.

*What have I gotten myself into? Will he have the patience to work with a French horn neophyte? Will he demand more of me than I have to give? Will he send me packing?*

The lights dim, and the music begins. When it comes to the horn solo in the third movement, Mr. Thornton plays it with such warm emotion and ethereal beauty that it completely banishes those troubling thoughts from my mind. Anyone who plays like that has to have a huge soul. He is no longer Mr. Thornton to me, but Michael, with a good chance to eventually become Mike.

As I have with other instruments, I check into the history of this new horn and find out that the valved horn was invented by a German, not a Frenchman. The Germans invented it, but the French got the naming rights. The Germans were not happy. This is but another example of the enmity between France and Germany. Except for a historically brief period of unification under Charlemagne in the Middle Ages, the two countries have battled each other militarily and culturally for centuries. Not until the end of WWII and the subsequent creation of NATO and the European Union have they lived with at least mutual tolerance.

Tracking the multi-faceted contests of France v. Germany through the ages makes for interesting scoreboard watching.

Let's start with what may matter the most to both countries, soccer. Since 1931 France has held a significant edge, winning fifteen games to Germany's nine, with eight draws. Scoreboard:

France 1

Germany 0

In the Napoleonic Wars of 1801-15, the victory went to France.

France 2

Germany 0

The Franco-Prussian War of 1870 was won by Germany.

France 2

Germany 1

The Second World War was not just France v. Germany, so we will leave that conflict out of the scoring. Turning to food and wine, the French win hands down.

France 3

Germany 1

But when it comes to music, there is no comparison. How can any country even come close to the German powerhouse lineup of Bach, Beethoven, Mendelssohn, Schuman, Strauss, Wagner, and Mahler? Throw in neighboring Austria with Mozart, Schubert, Brahms, and Bruckner, and it is the Germanic tribes by a landslide. The gap is so wide that the official scorer (me) awards two points to Germany

Final score:

France 3

Germany 3

The contest ends in a tie. It is a nice diplomatic balance of power.

Having dispelled my misgivings about studying with Michael Robert Thornton, driving down the highway to my first French horn lesson, I cannot help but think of the end piece already. A bit ahead of myself, to say the least, but having heard Mr. Thornton play the exquisite Tchaikovsky 5th symphony solo a week earlier, I have had visions of playing that piece myself.

When I meet Michael Robert Thornton, he immediately makes me feel at ease and, in fact, says how excited *he* is to be working with me and to be part of this unusual project. In no time at all, he is *Mike*.

Mike gives me some very simple exercises at our second lesson, and I get a little bored practicing them at home. To stay interested, I download the sheet music for the "Tchai Five" excerpt and work on it, too.

We continue to move slowly at the third lesson, and toward the end of it, I show Mike the sheet music. He blinks at me for a moment as if to say, "Are you kidding me?" Instead, he says, not unkindly, "OK, let's hear it."

I play it, not without mistakes, but I play it. Mike puts his hands on his hips, looks at me over his glasses, and after a pause, says, "That's not normal. I know you've had a few lessons on the trumpet and trombone, but Jim, that's not normal. You've only had the horn for two weeks!"

My abnormality notwithstanding, Mike is by no means letting me off the hook for learning how to play the horn properly. He is an excellent teacher and often demonstrates with metaphors. Some are theoretical, and some empirical. He talks about letting the breath flow as if I were releasing a bowling ball from my hand down the alley. I could not quite relate to that one. Instead, I picture a stream flowing smoothly over rocks, sustaining its flow evenly.

For one training exercise, he asks me to buy a kid's pinwheel and practice making it turn evenly with long, pinpoint breaths. That one helps a lot.

To correct my too-aggressive tonguing, he leads me into his kitchen. Turning on the tap, he takes his finger and moves it slowly through the column of water. It interrupts the flow. Then he moves his finger quickly through the stream, and the water appears to flow continuously. That also helps me a lot. A quick flick of the tip of my tongue against the hard palate just behind my teeth to articulate a note without breaking the tone is like the continuous flow of the water.

The more I practice, the smoother my playing becomes, but I still lack enough endurance to get through the entire Tchaikovsky excerpt cleanly. At the end of an hour and a half at most, my lips give out, and my breath produces a wavering tone.

A wavering tone on the horn is almost as uncomfortable to listen to as an aging soprano whose once thrilling and trilling vibrato has morphed into more of a high-pitched gargle.

Worse than a waver, though, is what horn players call cracking or clamming. It is sometimes due to a problem with the airflow and/or embouchure, but it often comes from the accumulation of condensation somewhere in those treacherously looped tubes.

Like a pipe smoker who is always fiddling with the tobacco in the bowl, tamping it down, knocking off burnt ash, and re-lighting it, the horn player is constantly draining the condensation from the eighteen feet of tubing coiled into the compact, round body of the instrument.

There are nine places where condensation can gather and make the horn crack. Trying to find just which one of these moisture traps is the guilty party can be like playing hide and seek. Open one valve and find not a drop. Try another, still dry. This can go on through all the nine possibilities, although there are two in particular that cause the problem more often than not, so that is where you start.

Some professional horns have a spit, or water release valve, as on the trumpet, but mine does not. Pulling out one curved tube after another and pushing them back into place in rather tight quarters clanks unmusically like a plumber rattling his wrenches under the bathroom sink.

According to *thetrumpetblog.com*, "The reason moisture (not spit) forms in all brass instruments is the fact that as the player forces warm air through the instrument, condensation forms on the inner walls and requires the player to dump the moisture from time to time. Feel your instrument. It always feels cool to the touch."[2]

When I practice for an hour or more, I dump a lot of moisture. After a while, it becomes a habit to pull out a tube and dump it in order to avoid cracking. At first, I spread a washcloth by my side on the floor, but it gets soggy, and even though I know it is not spit, I look for a different solution to moisture catching.

My father was an inveterate cigar smoker, and I inherited his vintage 1920s brass spittoon that he used quite regularly.

Spittoons have long gone the way of the hand crank telephone and Double-Handi washboard, but back in the day, you could find spittoons almost everywhere. They were in bars, of course, but also in homes, barbershops, offices, banks, and even churches, as Langston Hughes memorialized in his poem, "Brass Spittoons."

So, Dad's spittoon has a new life as the condensation catcher for my horn. When I empty the horn into the spittoon, it doesn't make a 'ping' sound as it does in the cartoons, but it is a somewhat droll accessory in my music room.

While Mike has agreed to work with me on the Tchaikovsky, his selection for the end piece is the horn solo in Brahms's *Symphony No. 3*. It is shorter but more challenging, at least for me. The dynamics are demanding, and unless you get them right, the excerpt sounds dull.

Visual imagery helps me get a sense of what Brahms wanted us to feel. I picture myself standing in the sand on the waterline of an ocean beach, facing the infinite horizon of the sea. The tide is coming in, and the wavelets wash over my feet and ankles, pushing them into the sand and toward the shore. But before the surge ends, the water reverses direction and pulls my feet back toward the ocean, sinking them deeper and deeper into the sand. It is as if, at that point in the changing tide, the water is uncertain whether it wants to rise or fall, ebb or flow.

And so it is with the Brahms *Symphony No. 3* excerpt.

There is a certain pulse moving it forward, but it does not

hook on to anything; it is ambiguous as to its destination. The music rises and falls uncertainly. Then it seems to make a decision to rejoice and to resolve the conflict calmly. But just as you think that is where Brahms is going, he ends the solo on a rising note, like a questioning raised eyebrow.

Analyzing a score in this fashion, phrase by phrase, and being able to play the emotion you discover is both demanding and rewarding. It is part of the hard work musicians put in before they ever set foot on a stage in a concert hall. Shakespearean actors dissect a play's script in a similar way, trying to find the truth behind the words on the page.

Mike regularly throws new music at me, mostly études. Playing études helps my technique so I can play the Tchaikovsky and Brahms better. They are designed to develop skills for a reliable embouchure, a steady column of air and air speed, long phrases, and dynamics.

As I improve, I begin to see how I might play something better, a phrase here, the quality of a note there, and feel that it is within my reach to do it. Mike has even used the word "refining" in talking about a passage in the Tchaikovsky or Brahms. He is actually coaching me now, coloring and molding the music into a sound that might evoke an emotional response.

Even more emotional than Brahms #3 or Tchaikovsky #5 is the short horn solo in the fourth movement of Brahms *Symphony No. 1*. It has such a graceful, heavenly quality that whenever I hear it, I have to stop what I am doing and just listen. Its power over me is, I am sure, also due to the fact that it was my mother's favorite phrase in all of music.

*Well, if I can play the Brahms 3 and Tchai 5 excerpts, why not the Brahms 1?* I go to download the sheet music from a British website and am baffled by what I see.

It seems that just as the Brits have different words than ours for various everyday things, their boot/our trunk, their bonnet/our hood, their spanner/our wrench, their bobby/our policeman, their flat/our apartment, so too do they have different words for musical notation. Their quaver is our eighth note; their crotchet is our quarter note.

Their terminology seems to be completely random compared to our very mathematical and easy-to-understand system. Some are counter-intuitive, such as the breve, which suggests brevity but is actually a whole note, the longest note you can put down on a page. Then there is my favorite term for the almost impossibly fast 164th note, worthy of a tongue twister contest at a county fair. It is the incomparable *semi-hemidemisemiquaver.* Enough said.

There is a charming tale behind the Brahms *Symphony No. 1* melody. It is said that as Brahms was trekking one day through the high meadows of the Swiss Alps, dressed as he would have been in those times, in sturdy boots, tweed trousers and jacket, perhaps a matching vest, a cravat, and a local narrow brim hat, he heard a shepherd playing a lovely tune on an alphorn. He was enchanted. Brahms took out his pocket notebook and wrote down the tune. It is the haunting melody the French horn plays in the fourth movement of his *Symphony No. 1.* Inspiration strikes unpredictably.

Mike and I are talking about this Brahmsian anecdote at a lesson one day, and he says, "Wait a minute, stay right there."

He disappears, his bare feet padding around a corner and out of earshot. He has already shown me part of his historical horn collection. One, a small, pocket hunting horn that looks like a miniaturized French horn complete with valves, that was used mostly by the Germans. They hunted primarily on foot and so liked the scaled-down size. Another in his collection is a large valve-less natural horn, which resembles a double hula-hoop, that the French preferred. It was worn around the mounted hunt master's neck, so he could grasp it easily as he galloped and sounded the call to the hounds.

What Mike reappears with is an alphorn, very much like the one Brahms would have seen and heard on his memorable hill walk, and almost the same as those played in the Austrian and Italian Alps.

The alphorn is big and long. The generally accepted length is 12 feet, give or take 7.4 inches, depending on whether you prefer the legendary explanation of its length or the modern one. Mike's alphorn is made of wood, as are all alphorns, and tapers from the cornucopia-shaped bell that rests on the ground on one end, to the small mouthpiece, way at the other end.

The story goes that in the old days, to get the right size alphorn, two men would go to the forest with a saw and look for a young pine tree growing crooked out of a steep hillside. They would hike and look until they found one to their liking. Then, and here comes the good part, one man would stand on the other man's shoulders and cut down the tree. Hence, the inexact give-or-take twelve-foot length. If Hans and Franz in Austria happened to be a little taller than Luigi and

Giovanni in Italy, then their alphorn would be a bit longer.

But the Swiss, being the Swiss, took an altogether different approach. Their penchant for precision, from watches to train schedules, led them to establish a national standard for an alphorn. It is exactly 3.47 meters, or to be just as precise, 11.38451 feet.

But here's the rub. That Swiss horn is 7.4 inches shorter than the generally accepted twelve feet. It suggests the twin hypotheses that either Swiss men are on average 7.4 inches shorter than the average Italian or Austrian, or that the Italians and Austrians always wore their green, three-cornered hat when they went alphorn hunting, but the Swiss did not.

Mike's alphorn is custom-made with his family crest carved into the bell. There are no valves, so you play different notes with subtle changes in your embouchure and the speed of the air you blow.

"Here, try it," offers Mike, as he hands me the alphorn.

I am transfixed and transported, no longer standing in Mike's suburban home's music studio but there with Brahms on a steep Swiss mountainside. And the music just flows. On the first try, I play the theme we've been working on, and on the alphorn, the sound is even more beguiling.

The alphorn experience stays with me, and I have a good week of practice on the standard French horn. The Tchaikovsky and even the more difficult Brahms #3 excerpts are coming along. When I see Mike for my next lesson, I pause after some warm-ups and wait for what he wants me to play next. He starts to say something but stops. He begins again and stops again. Then he says softly, "Play the Brahms

#3. Don't think about the notes. You know the notes; now play the music."

Even though I have taken one hundred and eight lessons on ten instruments, practiced over nine hundred hours, and heard those words before, hearing them this time rings true. There is such a difference between playing the notes and playing the music. The notes come from the pages on the music stand in front of you, while the music comes from something deep inside your soul. You have to be ready to receive wisdom. It is a quiet epiphany, and without putting words to it, I understand.

And so it is only at this moment, as I play the Brahms #3 on the French horn, that I actually feel the emotion I am trying to convey with my playing. I feel it because I can hear it. I am playing the music. It lifts and falls, soars and subsides. The tone is full and round, and the horn's melancholy richness fills the room. As the last note echoes and fades, without thinking and with my heart full of joy, I raise my horn in triumph.

# Finale

Writing this book took a little over three years. During that time, my musical world expanded exponentially, from my being an appreciative but casual listener to one who can play ten of the orchestral instruments in at least a reasonably listenable fashion and listen with greater purpose and intelligence to orchestral and chamber music.

That shift in my MI (Musical Intelligence) has made going to concerts and even listening to music on the radio an immeasurably richer experience. I can pick out the sounds of each instrument and understand what the musicians are doing to collectively deliver some of the most glorious music in history.

To me, it has been a confirmation that you cannot predict everything in life and that you are not done living until you have breathed your last breath. Both are good for you, body and soul.

Whatever we do in the present, we bring to bear on it the totality of all of our past experiences and memories. Whether it is conscious or subconscious, we are who we are because of all the things that have ever happened to us, large and small, that bring us to a particular moment in time. It is the sum of what we have done and not done: all the feelings we've embraced and the ones we denied, all that we have accomplished and where we have failed, the loves we have found and the ones we have lost, the ideals we have defended and those we walked away from, and the chances we took as well as the safety we preferred.

In acknowledging this truth, I realized at the end of three years that it was definitely more than a whim. Without knowing it, I had a vision, a clear one, and knew intuitively where to start. But I had to beware. A vision can be nothing more than a mind game that has you metaphorically gazing absently at the stars or counting daisies in a meadow, unless you have something to back it up.

When our kids were young, we encouraged them to follow their passion as they went through life, a popular parenting philosophy at the time. But we had a caveat. Follow your passion, yes, but get really, really, really, really good at it. Otherwise, the vision is nothing more than a dream.

If, however, you have a goal to go along with that vision, and a strategy of how to achieve that goal, then you can make something happen.

My vision was to write a book. My goal to fulfill that vision was to play all the instruments in the orchestra. My strategy to reach the goal was to take lessons. One dovetails right into the other, and they become inseparable. Their interdependence is so strong that if you take one away, the whole thing collapses, like breaking one leg off a three-legged stool. But all of this was subconscious.

It is a bit odd, given the nature of this book, but to follow my vision and achieve my goal, I subconsciously was developing something akin to a business plan. Absolutely without a conscious thought, I was doing what I had done many times earlier in my life. As the legendary Negro League and Major League Baseball pitcher Satchel Paige is reputed to have said, "Never look back; your past may be catching up on you."

Most projects do not take three years to complete, so to do it, there had to be a rock-solid commitment and unwavering discipline to see it through. When you work for a company or a large organization, you are in a hierarchical environment with support staff, co-workers, and bosses. In this equation, discipline and commitment are often externally motivated. There is pressure from above and below, and competition from alongside to do your job well. There is nothing inherently wrong with that structure, although the company or organization is often the greater beneficiary of it rather than you.

When you are working by yourself at home, without any external structure, the situation is entirely different. It all has to come from inside you. What is it that made me, a non-musician, practice for hours a day almost every day for three years? It was desire. I wanted to do it.

The simple fact that I wanted to do it was a profound motivator. Whenever my commitment or discipline was in danger of flagging, I reminded myself that this was something I wanted to do. That thought has helped others, too. When a friend complained to me about his job, I reminded him that he wanted that job and that he should understand that there were bound to be obstacles along the way. But an obstacle is not a stop sign. It is a detour sign. It doesn't keep you from reaching your destination; it just means you have to find a new way to get there.

I found that to be applicable in my working with ten different music teachers, each one with a distinct personality and approach to teaching. Since no two were alike, I more or less had to learn how to learn in ten different ways. The road to playing a classical excerpt always had detour signs on it, and the detour I took with one teacher didn't necessarily work as well with another.

I had teachers who were men, women, straight, gay, Chinese, Japanese, married, divorced, youngish, and oldish. Yet, if I were putting together a team of music teachers, I could not assemble a better roster. The diversity was stimulating, and it brought different, valuable insights from their disparate experiences and pedagogy to my musical education. I came with a certain degree of knowledge, then built on that knowledge with instruction, practice, and feedback, with that loop continuing again and again. Each time I circled back to the beginning, the loop got bigger and bigger, encompassing more knowledge, more instruction, better practicing, and more helpful feedback until I was able to play a challenging piece of music.

Input coming from so many different directions was an instructional bouillabaisse, and my job was to be able to identify all the separate ingredients and understand how, when combined in a certain way, they came together to make something greater than the sum of its parts.

What I figured out was that I had to be flexible and believe in and trust whomever I was working with at the time, unless they proved to be unworthy of that trust. To my dismay, that actually happened twice, and I had to change teachers midstream. I did it reluctantly, but I was not going to sacrifice the success of the overall project once I was pretty certain that I would not reach my goal with my current teacher.

I loved working in education years ago, but I could never understand why schools were so slow to dismiss a teacher who, almost from the start, clearly was not a good fit for the job. Typically, a school will give a teacher at least two years before even considering cutting them loose. It is a very kind and compassionate approach the way a school will counsel a teacher on where they need to improve and give them a year to make the changes. Then comes a warning for another year, until finally, their contract is not renewed—a nice way of saying you are fired. All that wasted time when the school knew after six months that the teacher was not good. Schools forget that the overall goal is to educate their students, and if they stick with a teacher after they know the teacher is not up to the task, they are doing the students a grave disservice.

Keeping in mind what is most important in the big picture is central to not getting lost in too many suffocating details. As Mike Thornton told me in playing the French horn, "You know the notes, now play the music."

Of course, getting to that point takes a great deal of effort. What helped me through the hardest periods of learning all the instruments was a certain positive spirit and thinking of the journey as a musical adventure.

True to most adventures, at the start of one, you sally forth, not knowing exactly what will happen next. As you make a path through the tangles and continue on your way, you realize that you can exalt in your small accomplishments and successes, and that momentum helps push you past the frustration

At the beginning of the book, I wrote about *process* people and *results* people, hoping that each faction would find a loosening of their boundaries and, if not plunge, at least wade into somewhat deeper and unknown waters on the other side, with an adventurous spirit.

It really does not take much to be an adventurer. You do not have to make a first descent in a kayak down a remote river, hike the entire length of the Appalachian Trail, or ride a camel across the Sahara Desert. All it takes to be an adventurer is a willingness to try something that you have never done before. It can be as big as changing careers, moving to a new place to live, learning a language, or as small as taking up golf. Some may seem commonplace or even mundane, but they are adventures, nonetheless. If you have never done it before and decide to do it, you are embarking on an adventure.

I don't consider myself to be an extraordinary person. But by my definition, I am an adventurer. Throughout my life, if I wanted something, I went after it. I did not have to know how to do whatever it was before I started. If I sensed a resonance with an idea, I found out how to do it, either ahead of time or along the way.

I have been an actor in New York, a sales manager for a ski and tennis company, a cowboy, and a wilderness outfitter. I have run a national advertising agency, been an educator, and co-founded an NGO to build schools for girls in Afghanistan. The only one of those experiences that I had any training for was acting.

It did not take courage or self-confidence to do all those things. It did take an acceptance of not knowing all the answers beforehand or exactly where things would end up. But that was secondary to going after something I wanted to do. And if you nurture that spirit of adventure, it doesn't have to ever end. It doesn't have to fade with your youth, nor when you marry, nor when your waist is wider than your shoulders. You can keep it when your hair turns grey, or even when your ears, teeth, and eyes are on the nightstand by your bed.

I was successful and accomplished enough doing all the things I did to retire for the first time at fifty-four, and, like results people, that satisfied the side of my personality that wanted measurable outcomes.

The journey, so important to process people, was equally satisfying. Delving into the worlds of business, wilderness guiding, education, the theatre, international aid, and lastly, music has left an indelible impression and given me a very gratifying life.

Remember, I started this project when I was seventy-six, so wherever you are on your life's path, I am betting that there is something within your reach that will bring you as much joy and fulfillment as this book has brought to me.

# Afterword

Not surprisingly, some things have changed since I started on this book. For one, I am now 80, not 76.

Those are just numbers, but other non-lineal things have changed as well.

In the time since I wrote in Chapter Seven about accepting as fact that our grown children would never marry their long-time partners, Liza and Dan not only got married but followed it up by producing a son.

My strong attraction to the cello, which prompted me to continue lessons even while taking on a succession of other instruments, ended not with a bang but a whimper. After two and a half years, I could not tame the beast. It was disheartening to realize that after only twelve lessons on the flute, oboe, trumpet, and French horn, I could play them better than after all that time on the cello.

At the same time, I realized that wind instruments and I got along very well, and I decided after finishing the book to continue my musical life with the clarinet. I chose it because, like so many things we learn in our formative years, the lessons I took on the clarinet sixty-seven years ago have stuck. My fingers instinctively know where to go, my embouchure is automatic, and my ability to follow the dynamics and craft musical phrases with emotion is intuitive. With practice and lessons, I think I will be able to play with others at a level it would take years to achieve on any of the other instruments.

When I was a kid, there was an early TV show, in black and white, called "Life Begins at Eighty." Ordinary people told stories about what they were doing with their life in their eighties. I thought then that they were so old, almost pathetic; why bother watching? But there was also something curiously fascinating about them. Now I know that if we are lucky and still have our health and wits about us, living is just as fulfilling and vibrant as at any stage of life.

Memories are for the past. Dreams are for the future. I am extremely fortunate to have an abundance of both.

# Acknowledgements

To my early readers and fellow writers Carol Samson and Gene Hayworth for seeing enough in those early sketches to say, "Write on."

To my incredible teachers who took on the risk of trying to teach a septuagenarian how to play their beloved instrument and who, in the process, became my friends: Byron Dudrey (double bass), Chris Abbot (cello), Pricilla Arasaki (violin), Cathy Peterson (flute), Peter Cooper (oboe), Roger Soren (bassoon), Jon Stubbs (trombone), Ryan Gardner (trumpet), and Michael Robert Thornton (French horn).

To Cindy Low, who, between bites of a Florentine omelet, gave me the title of this book.

To Rob Smith, who never lets me get away with anything.

For being taken on by the first and only publisher I showed the book to, I am happy to have run across Anthony Paustian, of Bookpress Publishing, at a book festival.

To my editor at Bookpress, Susan Holden Martin, who, lucky for me, loves the details.

# Notes

[1] Banzhoff, S., Del Mar Ropero, M., Menzel, G., Salmen, T., Gross, M., Caffier, PP. *Medical Issues in Playing the Oboe: A Literature Review.* Med Probl Perform Art. 2017 Dec; 32(4):235-246. doi: 10.21091/mppa.2017.4040. PMID: 29231958.

[2] Chidester, B. (2016, April 27). *Good Trumpet Players Are Full of Hot Air* [web log]. Retrieved from http://www.thetrumpetblog.com /good-trumpet-players-are-full-of-hot-air/#:~:text=The%20reason %20moisture%20(not%20spit,moisture%20from%20time%20to% 20time.